PRIVATE INVESTIGATING

Made Easy

Private Investigating Made Easy

How To Conduct Investigations Using Public Records And More!

by Kelly E. Riddle
Licensed Private Investigator

Published by
Historical Publications
15705 Hilcroft Cove
Austin, Texas 78717-5331

ISBN # 1-881825-05-1

Foreword

Kelly E. Riddle is a licensed Private Investigator and the owner of Kelmar and Associates private investigations in San Antonio, Texas. As a former police officer, expertise was developed as a SWAT team member, investigator and training officer. His education includes a Bachelor of Science in Criminal Justice from the University of North Alabama. With more than 15 years of investigative experience, he has developed the quickest and easiest methods to research records and conduct investigations. At the onset of his private investigative career, he made the decision to only obtain records and conduct investigations utilizing "public records and information". Because of this approach to investigating and the knowledge acquired through years of experience, anyone can now have the easy, step-by-step instructions to research records, locate subjects and perform inquiries, simply by following the information in this book.

The detailed information in this book will provide the reader with the necessary tools to:

- Check a person's criminal history
- Check a person's civil history
- Check a person's credentials
- Locate old friends, classmates, or military buddies
- Locate minors
- Locate hidden insurance policies
- Locate ex-spouses who owe child support
- Locate the owners of a business
- Locate hidden assets
- Conduct background investigations
- Determine a person's financial status
- Determine a person's marital status
- And much more!

Contents

Introduction

Since the early 1950's, the improvements in record keeping by the government have forever changed the ability to keep one's personal information a secret. Through the use of computers, more information on an individual can be compiled and easily accessed. The majority of professional private investigators have learned the art of accessing the abundant information that exists out there. However, unlike the stereo-types and the T.V. shows, most PI's do not obtain information illegally, nor do they obtain information that they should not legally have. The typical PI has a family and lives in a nice neighborhood just like the average person. They are not interested in going to jail for obtaining illegal information and being away from their families, especially when the information can only make them a small amount of money.

Although all good PI's know police officers, bankers and other people in the business community, seldom do these sources ever provide information to PI's. For example, all police departments have access to a computer which provides criminal records on subjects and is called the "N.C.I.C." records. This computer system receives information from all of the law enforcement agencies throughout the United States. Although this computer is the quickest way to check a person's criminal records, it is not always the best. The N.C.I.C. information is overseen by the Federal Bureau of Investigation (FBI), and they have started an intense effort to catch those law enforcement officials who sell or use the information for a purpose outside of their law enforcement functions. Besides police officers refusing to check the N.C.I.C. computer for PI's because of the fear of imprisonment, the information is not always current or complete. It is not uncommon to find arrest information in other records which for one reason or another, never made it to the N.C.I.C. computer. Secondly, PI's have to provide information which they can testify to in a court of law. If information obtained cannot be documented and shown that it was legally obtained, the PI and their source could face criminal charges. In addition, PI's provide the information for a client who pays good money for information they can use. These clients do not want their businesses or themselves involved in any scandals.

The information obtained by PI's is obtained through sources and records which are accessible to the public. The reason for private investigators is simple: most people do not have the expertise to locate the proper records and/or the time. A majority of the records discussed in this book can be searched by computers in the PI's office. The general public does not qualify for these computer connections and therefore has to call the offices or go to them to conduct the searches. The records, however, are open to the public — if you know where they are, how to access them properly and what the records contain. The investigators that are employed in law enforcement agencies are too busy to assist the average person with personal matters. The need for personal assistance and a more in depth investigation helped create the private investigative industry. Even though police officers have a lot of "power", the general public does not realize that the officer does not have immediate access to half of the information a PI, or for that matter, the general public has. Most police officers have access to criminal records, driver's license records, motor vehicle records, and utility records. As you will see, the PI and the general public have access to a tremendous amount of other records. The information covered in this book provides the average person with the easiest methods to research records, any minimal costs which apply, and easy step by step instructions on investigating and obtaining pertinent information.

Disclaimer: Although the information discussed is available to the general public, care and caution should be maintained concerning the uses of the information. In addition, this information is intended for a person who has personal data that needs to be researched. Each state has a State Board that regulates private investigators and certain requirements must be met before you can investigate records or another party. For example, it is generally illegal for a person to provide an investigation (record search, surveillance, etc.) for someone else in exchange for money/profit unless they are licensed by the state as a private investigator.

Although you may seldom need the ability to research the records that we will discuss, the ability to do so will open several doors. In this day and age, a person should be aware of the type of person they are doing business with, the type of person they are about to marry, the abilities and qualifications of their doctor and other similar situations. It may even be interesting to see how simple it is for someone else to check you out!

Conflict of Interest? I remember a case that we worked in which the ability to research records confirmed the suspicions of our client. Our agency was approached by a trucking company who suspected a Vice-President of having a separate trucking company on the side. The client had a strict conflict of interest policy and therefore needed sufficient information in which to approach the subject. Because of the urgency, I traveled to the city in question and utilized the record searches described in this book. Through these records, I followed a "paper trail" which resulted in documents being obtained confirming the client's suspicions. The subject did own a separate company and was using the client's trucks to haul his trailers between Mexico and the U.S. The assumed name records provided the name of the subject's company, the business address, and other useful information. The deed records provided listings concerning ownership of property associated with the business, as well as other questionable practices. From these records sprung a wealth of supporting documents which concluded a successful investigation.

CHAPTER ONE

How to Get Started — General Pointers

When conducting record searches, there are certain factors which should be considered. For example:

Spelling — although you may already know the way the subject correctly spells their name, always check other common spellings. It is not uncommon to have the person entering the information in the records to be in a hurry and misspell a name. For example: the name Gonzales is often spelled Gonzalez (with a "Z"), or a letter may be left out (Kennedy may be Kenedy).

Initials — always check those listings by initials. Some computer programs only allow a certain number of letters (characters) to be entered on the screen. A name like Alexander Salvatierra may be listed as "A. Salvatierra". Also, the subject may have, for one reason or another, switched to signing documents utilizing only an initial.

Nick-Names — consider the possibility that the person entering the information knew the subject. Although the person's name may be Alexander, they sometimes went by "Junior" or "Alex" or some other name because their father is also named Alexander. In this day of increased gangs, it is not uncommon for a gang member to have another name given to them by their gang. If the person writing the report or entering the information in the records knew the subject by these other names, the records may be accessed only through the use of these other names (or alias).

Middle-Names — search by middle names because the subject may use this when trying to conceal information. They may have suddenly decided that they like their middle name better, or as previously stated, uses their middle name due to a relative with the same first name.

Maiden Names — search the records utilizing a woman's maiden name as subjects often revert back to this name when hiding or concealing information.

Divorcee Names — always check records by any names that the female may have obtained during a prior marriage. It is common for subjects to use these names in times of trouble.

Hyphenated-Names — because of the increase in the number of women who marry and keep their maiden name, or a child caught in a custody battle, all of the names must be checked. Additionally, a person may decide to maintain their maiden name in an effort to keep in touch with their ethnic or religious heritage. This is also commonly done for business reasons because a minority who married someone outside of their ethnic background can continue to use their maiden name to apply for grants and open other minority related opportunities. As an example, a name like Linda Ortiz-Daniels should be researched using the full name, as well as Linda Ortiz and Linda Daniels.

Business-Names — always check for businesses associated with a subject's name. For example, if you are checking records for a John Hernandez, always look for businesses under the name of Hernandez, such as Hernandez and Sons Moving Company, Hernandez Automotive or Hernandez and Associates.

Street Names — always check for different spellings for a street, as well as for other streets with the same name. As large cities annex smaller suburbs, it is common to find the same street name in different parts of the city. Double-check the direction associated with the street. For example, make sure you look up North 6th, East 5th or similar listings. In addition, pay attention to whether the street you are looking for is a road, street, avenue, boulevard, highway, farm road, etc.

Zip Codes — use the zip codes associated with an address to your benefit. Recognize that most people stay around or come back to the area they live or feel safe in. If you have located a number of possibilities where a subject may be, start by searching those in the same zip code or surrounding zip codes. Also, remember that most telephone books now list the zip code along with the street and telephone number.

Foster Names — if a subject is known to have been a foster child and the names of the foster parents are known, search utilizing their last name if it is different than your subject's name.

Surrounding Communities — consider checking records in nearby counties, large cities, or states. It is not uncommon for a couple to marry in a nearby county or state due to more lenient rules. In addition, the cost of opening a business (licenses, fees, taxes, etc.) may be cheaper in a nearby state.

Types of Record Searches — records can be searched by various methods. The amount of funds available to the county, state or government agency has a direct bearing on the method in which you will be able to conduct the search. Most offices now have at least one computer terminal available for the public to use along with a sheet nearby which provides simple instructions. A microfiche machine may be used as well. This looks similar to a computer screen and has a light which shines through the plastic microfiche and projects the information onto the screen. A nearby collection of microfiche (which are usually dark blue pieces of plastic with writing on it) are usually arranged in alphabetical order. You can find the microfiche that indicates names similar to the one you desire and place it in the slide-out part of the machine. By inserting the microfiche, the information is projected on the screen. The records may also be searched manually by looking through indexes (books) which are alphabetically arranged. In some cases, records can be searched by calling a special telephone number for the office, which will then give you instructions on how to search the record over the phone using your key pad on the telephone to enter the name. This is usually a free search, as are all the other methods listed. Sometimes, you may have to check two or three of these methods, depending on what year you need to review and when the system was converted to a computer.

Courthouse Offices — the majority of the records we will be discussing are located in the county courthouse. The county clerk's office, the county district clerk's office and the tax assessor's office generally oversee the records. There may be several departments within these offices. As an example, the county clerk's office may have the civil section, the criminal section, assumed names section, deed records section and various other departments. Although the word "county" is used in this book, some states denote a county by other names. For example, Louisiana refers to their counties as a "Parish", while New York calls them a "Borough". This does not change the information available, only how you ask directory assistance for the local telephone number.

The courthouse records and their locations should be fully understood to be properly used. The records are under the direction of certain court clerks. The following is designed to assist you in understanding this structure.

Courthouse Offices

District Court Clerk	County Court Clerk	Tax Assessor
1. Criminal records	1. Civil records	1. Vehicle taxes
2. Civil records	2. Criminal records	2. Property taxes
A. Divorces	3. Assumed names	3. Business taxes
B. Delinquent debts	4. Deed records	
C. Delinquent taxes	5. Birth records	
D. Property damages	6. Financing statements	
E. Personal damages	7. Marriage records	
F. Judgements	8. Tax liens	
	9. Grantor/grantee indexes	
	10. Livestock brand indexes	

It may be helpful to think of the system in comparison to the airline industry's "hub system". The airlines have certain cities that act as the hub of a wheel, or the primary overseer of the flights in their area. Each hub has the ability to direct, oversee, alter and restrict flights under their direction. Likewise, the court clerks in the courthouse oversee the processing, additions to, storage and retrieval of records under their authority. Although there are a lot of records available, only two or three clerks oversee the information. When you enter a courthouse, you should focus on locating the offices of these clerks. Once their offices are found, you can easily locate the appropriate indexes.

Copies of Courthouse Records — while searching the records, if you find something that you need a copy of, you can usually print this from your computer onto a nearby computer printer for a nominal fee ($.05 — $.10 cents each). A clerk can advise you how to do this and what the charge per page is. If the record is in a file and is already a part of a document, check with the clerks. Most courthouses have a copier accessible to the public and charge a nominal fee per page.

Social Security Prefixes — the first three numbers of a person's social security number will identify which state the number was issued in. Additional searches may be necessary in this state if it is different from the one you are in. A list of these prefixes are provided as follows:

AREA NO.	STATE	AREA NO.	STATE
001-003	New Hampshire	433-439	Louisiana
004-007	Maine	440-448	Oklahoma
008-009	Vermont	449-467	Texas
010-034	Massachusetts	468-477	Minnesota
035-039	Rhode Island	478-485	Iowa
040-049	Connecticut	486-500	Missouri
050-134	New York	501-502	N. Dakota
135-158	New Jersey	503-504	S. Dakota
159-211	Pennsylvania	505-508	Nebraska
212-220	Maryland	509-515	Kansas
221-222	Delaware	516-517	Montana
223-231	Virginia	518-519	Idaho
232-236	W. Virginia	520	Wyoming
237-246	N. Carolina	521-524	Colorado
247-251	S. Carolina	525,585	N. Mexico
252-260	Georgia	526-527	Arizona
261-267	Florida	528-529	Utah
268-302	Ohio	530	Nevada
303-317	Indiana	531-539	Wash.
318-361	Illinois	540-544	Oregon
362-386	Michigan	545-573	Calif.
387-399	Wisconsin	574	Alaska
400-407	Kentucky	575-576	Hawaii
408-415	Tennessee	577-579	D. C.
416-424	Alabama	580	Virgin I.
425-428	Mississippi	581-585	P. Rico
429-432	Arkansas	586	Guam

Additions:

586	American Samoa	586	Phillipines
588	Mississippi	602-626	Calif.
589-595	Florida	627-645	Texas
596-599	Puerto Rico	646-647	Utah
600-601	Arizona	648-649	N. Mexico
700-728	Railroad		

Attitude — always assume that you have the right to the information you are searching. Certain counties may restrict some records from the public for reasons of security (example: birth records may be restricted to protect the privacy of the birth parents in adoption cases). Even though the governmental agency which oversees the records in question allow the public to search their records, they sometimes may try to discourage this practice. Therefore, you should approach the record searches with an aggressive and a positive attitude. If you proceed as if you know what you're doing (as if you have done it before), you often times will not be confronted or denied access. Persistence may be needed, as the clerk's may not be eager to assist you.

CHAPTER TWO

Locating Subjects

Locating the Missing Son: I received a call from a mother whose son was on the Honor Roll at school, in ROTC and was preparing to enter the Navy in two months after he graduated. She indicated that their relationship had deteriorated and his teachers advised that her son's grades were slipping, primarily due to a lack of attendance. Just prior to the call, the mother had concluded that her son had moved out and the navy recruiter was concerned that the subject would not complete the testing required to fulfill the contract and enter the Navy as scheduled. Starting with the recruiter, I found out that the subject was seeing a girl, although all that was known was a first name. I then contacted the ROTC Commander at the high school and some of the teachers who were able to tell me who the subject's friends were. Although the friends were reluctant to provide much information, I did find out the girlfriend's last name. With this, I went to work checking records for all property owned by subjects with the same last name. Then, I narrowed this down to the ZIP code in which the public high school was located. The records immediately began to point to several distinct possibilities which I continued to research through public records. It resulted in locating the girlfriend, who was hiding the subject because he had changed his mind about entering the military out of fear that his girlfriend wouldn't wait for him.

The success in locating someone has a lot to do with how much personal information you know about the subject. For example, if the person's name is John Smith and the middle name, date of birth, social security number, or other pertinent information is unknown, the search will take longer and be more difficult due to the numerous Smith's, J. Smith's, John Smith's, Johnnie Smith's and associated spellings. Always check other common spellings, nick-names, maiden names or business names when conducting a search. For instance, the last name of Kennedy can be spelled with one or two "N's" (Kennedy or Kenedy). The name Gonzales can be spelled Gonzales or Gonzalez. Never assume that the most common spelling is correct and never assume that the spelling was entered correctly in the records.

Let's assume that you need to locate a subject and have very little information on the subject. First, check the obvious. Call the local telephone operator (dial 1411) and determine any listings for the subject. Be sure that you ask for the address and telephone number. Although you probably have access to a telephone book, a check with directory assistance should be conducted to see if there are any new listings since the telephone book was published. Secondly, check with directory assistance for the spouse of the subject. It is a common practice for those who are trying to hide to use their spouses names. If neither of these provide any information, check for any initials (Example: J. Smith for John Smith), a maiden name or a nick-name. If you suspect that the subject has moved to a particular street but don't know the house number, you can ask the operator if they have any listings for a "Smith" on Clark St. (or the appropriate street name). This is a good way to find out that the subject has relatives on the street that they may or may not be staying with. Once the information is obtained, there are several methods to determine if this is the same subject and these methods will be addressed later in this book.

Old telephone books may be a good source of information as the telephone company only provides telephone numbers on recent listings. If old books are available, you should check for the subject and relatives and use the information to get started or confirm other information.

Another quick reference which is generally easily accessible is a local city-directory such as the Polk's City Directory or the local Criss-Cross Directory. These books are compiled for the business community and are used for marketing and sales purposes. The books are put together for a particular city and list the residents in alphabetical order. These books can be found at a library, city hall, the courthouse, or most businesses and are free to use. When a name is found, the listings provide their employer or trade (Example: General Motors or Painter), their address and a telephone number. The books have a separate section where you can look up the street name and the house number. This will tell you the occupant of the house, their telephone number, their neighbors and their respective telephone numbers, as well as the nearest intersection. The books also indicate symbols which tell you if the person is the owner of the house, a new resident, etc. A third listing in the book allows you to search and determine who a telephone number is listed to. For example, the number 657-5555 would be looked up by first finding the prefix (657) and then the remaining numbers (5555). Once the number is found, the person who the number is listed to can be determined. After the name is identified, you can then "criss-cross" the directory and check the name under the name directory to get their address and employer. Then the street address can be checked to determine the

City Directory Listings

WOODLAWN AV W - FROM 1600 MAIN AV WEST BEY CITY LIMITS

- **ZIP CODE 78212**
- N FLORES INTERSECTS

606 Vacant
607 Vacant
611 Martinez Richd T [9] + ●
614 Vacant
615 Arevalos Henry G [9] + ●
621 SERAPHIC FRANCISCAN SISTERS CONVENT 734 3364
630 SAINT FRANCIS NURSING HOME 736 3177
631 Cordova [2]
635 Vacant
639 Not Verified

- RIPLEY AV INTERSECTS

700 Villegas Fortunato R [9] + ●
701★Mora Atslias & Martha ● 736 0513
706 Tondre Lorene B [9] + ● 736 3049
710 Morgan G [3]
711 Not Verified
714 Valdez L Z & Clemencia [9] + ● 733 7115
717 Vacant
719 Not Verified
721 Vacant
723 Crail Jas H Jr [7]
734 Vacant

- I&GNRR CROSSES

737 Clauss Marvin L [9] + ● 735 0755
738 Rodriguez Daniel G & Norma C [9] + ● 733 0744

- AGANIER AV INTERSECTS

802★Salas Richd
804 Ingmundson Paul T & Conneen B [8] ● 732 0029
805 Not Verified
806★Bernal Lois B & Maria L ● 735 4685
811 Rodriguez Joe [2]
814 Hid Estela [2] 736 5528
815 Hernandez Manuel T & Uoliria G [3] ● 733 3548
816 Apartments
 1 Not Verified
 2 Espinoza Christina L [2]
 3-4 Vacant (2 Apts)
 5 Ramos Alberto [3]
 6 Pimentel Luis P [3]
817a Hernandez Ruben [6]
817b Vacant
818 Not Verified
821 Vacant
821b Gutierrez Eloy F [8] ● 735 1682
822 Not Verified
826 Bell Ralph L & Maradee W [6] ● 732 9340
827 Not Verified
830 Rodriguez Socorro [9] + ● 734 9497
831★Dominguez Lily
832-835 Not Verified (2 Hses)
 Kurtz [3]
836 Not Verified
Rear Vacant

- BLANCO RD INTERSECTS
- **ZIP CODE 78201**

900 De Leon Sebastian [9] + ● 733 1261
901★Roop Ronald
910 Maldonado Jesse & Adelina C [9] + ● 734 0976
 Maldonado Dan E 734 0976
 Maldonado David A 734 0976
912 Not Verified
916 Rivas Alfredo C & Consuelo S [9] + ● 736 5476

h HOUSEHOLDER

Smith Jennifer h8916 Data Point Dr Apt 2001
Smith Jennifer sls assoc American Uniform
Smith Jerline h822 Pleasure Park 673 6374
Smith Jerraldyn E legal asst Banks h11406 Destiny Dr
Smith Jerrel F & Margt, cabinet wkr h139 Shady Rill St ●
Smith Jerry h4100 Parkdale St Apt 3121 614 4272
Smith Jerry Jr & Nicky, bldr h1234 Shadow Elm Woods ●
Smith Jerry H h7531 Greenbelt Dr ● 680 2024
Smith Jerry Jay Rev & Betty J, admn ofcr United Methodist Ch h222 Clearview Dr ● 432 5281
Smith Jerry K & Donna M USAF h6331 Ridge Pl ● 523 6658
Smith Jerry L & Irene R, civ serv wkr Lackland A F B h7315 Havenbrook St ● 673 4803
Smith Jerry W mgr criminal justice prog Alamo Area Council Regl Serv
Smith Jerry W & Sharon A (Jerry Smith Bldg Dev) h11810 Kellers Point ● 492 3330
Smith Jerry W Builder Developer (Jerry W Smith) 3003 NW Loop 410 Suite 203 349 3795
Smith Jesse prop mgr The Crossroads Pointe Apts r6014 Blanco Rd Apt 106
Smith Jesse L retd r4939 Zulema St 435 1052
Smith Jessie A retd h1605 Santa Anna St ● 734 8384
Smith Jim & Shirley, comp analyst I B M h7906 Misty Park ● 680 6903
Smith Jim h7110 Wurzbach Rd 615 0941
Smith Jim O & Joyce A, slsmn h5427 Billington St ● 349 2820
Smith Joan exec sec Greater S A Chamber of Commerce
Smith Jean K recpt El Hidalgo Law Offices h6325 Babcock Rd 696 6721
Smith Joan L prof dir Univ of Texas h12423 Wandering Trail 691 1668
Smith Joe h12221 Blanco Rd 377 2609
Smith Joe h1700 Jackson Keller Rd
Smith Joe & Yolanda h6743 Peachtree Dr (LV) ● 684 5444
Smith Joe E h10415 Annapolis Dr ● 696 1548
Smith Joe E pres J E S Inc
Smith Joe M h6020 Danny Kaye Dr 614 6587
Smith John h8003 Airflight St 647 8754
Smith John & Florine W; retd h6211 Birch Valley Dr ● 674 2855
Smith John h8922 Melinda Ct 681 8208
Smith John h1200 Patricia St 366 0392
Smith John h1400 Patricia St
Smith John A & Thelma, retd h6304 El Verde Rd (LV) ● 684 1149
Smith John A & Norma A, lwyr 115 E Travis Rm 320 h2382 W Woodlawn Av ● 435 6075
Smith John Aaron studt r3382 W Woodlawn Av 435 6075
Smith John B & Gail, tchr Lackland A F B h5818 Fawn Valley ● 673 2214
Smith John B & Marie A, cook Warm Springs r543 Thompson Pl 923 8314
Smith John C & Sandra F, mgr Checker Cab Co Inc h14015 Red Clover ● 492 3489
Smith John F & K, emp IBM h426 Woodway Forest ●
Smith John H dir Veterans Admn Day Treatment Cntr r5826 Cary Grant
Smith John M & Karen; mgr Chief Auto Parts h14911 Hidden Glen Woods ● 492 5019

owner of the house and the neighbors. With this information, you may want to confirm that the subject is the same one you are looking for and this can be done by various methods which will be discussed later in this book.

Consider checking the Post Office for a forwarding address. You can write or call the post office to request their form. They will only release the information if the information is requested on the Post Office's own form. Request the "Freedom of Information Act" form for determining a "change of address". This information is obtainable by the public under the Freedom of Information Act, section 352.643 of the Administrative Support Manual. If you desire to obtain the information in the quickest way possible, you should go directly to the post office. You have to go to the post office which handles the mail for the address in question.

To determine the post office that you need, call a post office (if there is more than one in the city) and ask them which station handles the street in question. Confirm the zip code and then ask for the address of the post office which handles the street/zip code in question. Proceed to the post office during normal working hours and ask one of the clerks for the previously mentioned form. You can complete the form in approximately 1-2 minutes and then return it to the clerk with a fee of $3.00. The clerk will then check their records for a forwarding address and provide you with the same. To do this, you have to know the "last known address", the zip code, and the person's name. This, along with the $3.00 fee will provide the current address if the person filed a change of address when they moved. The change of address tells the post office to send their mail to their new address.

The next place to search is the Public Utilities. Depending on the policies of the electric company or the water system which provides the services in your community, this information may or may not be accessible to the public. The majority of these departments have policies allowing their customers to

Freedom of Information Act Form

POSTMASTER

DATE ______________________

Under the "Freedom of Information Act", as per Section 352.643 of the Administrative Support Manual please furnish a change of address for the following:

______________________ NAME

______________________ LAST KNOWN ADDRESS

______________________ ZIP CODE

______________________ SIGNATURE OF REQUESTER

______________________ ADDRESS

______________________ CITY AND STATE

FOR POSTAL USE ONLY

RECEIPT # ______________________

NEW ADDRESS ______________________

____

CLERK ______________________

complete a request denying the general public from accessing their individual account. Therefore, most departments have a policy allowing the public access to the records. However, it is not unusual for the department to require you to request the information in writing along with the reason for the search. Each department has different rules governing the release of the information and you will therefore have to call and check their policy. The computer program that the departments use also determines whether they can search by name, address, social security number or all three. These searches are usually conducted free of charge, but may take one to three weeks.

A common record search is the Voter's Registration records. Every person who votes in any election must be registered to do so through the county's voters registration office. This office is usually located in the county courthouse or a nearby building. Depending on the policy of the department, you may be able to call in and have the search done, or you may be required to do so yourself in person. You can conduct the search by name and this is especially effective right before or after a major election. If you find a listing, you can request to see the actual record which will have the person's address and date of birth on it. Depending on the county, they may have a social security number and an employer listed.

The county's civil records may be worth reviewing to determine whether or not the subject has been sued or is suing anyone. If the person is being sued, the records will indicate where the sheriff's department served the subject with the citation (gave the subject the papers advising them that they were being sued). There are two different courts that handle civil records and are typically the district court clerk for the county and the county court clerk. The district court clerk handles cases that involve a higher degree of money, divorce cases, etc. The county clerk usually handles lawsuits involving damages under $1,000. Both of the court clerk's records should be searched and may be done by telephone, depending on their policy. If you are required to search these records in person, there should be no charge unless you request a copy. In divorce cases, child support, inheritance disputes, automobile accident cases, and others, you may find information listed in the file concerning relatives, friends, former addresses, employers, and property owned by the subject.

The county's criminal records may be another source of information. As in the civil records, the records are divided into the district criminal records and the county criminal records, depending on the severity of the criminal charge. These records are usually housed at the courthouse, and are open to the public at no charge (unless you request a copy) and can often be searched by calling into the office. If a listing is found, the file itself may be obtained from the clerk for review. Information in the file may indicate when the subject is scheduled to be in court (if the case is pending) and you may be able to locate and identify the subject when they arrive for the trial. It may also tell who their relatives, friends and employers are, as well as their probation officer (if on probation).

The county's Appraisal District records are a tremendous source of information and are usually located in or near the courthouse. The job of the Appraisal District is to oversee all of the property in a particular county and to determine the value of the property for taxes. Generally speaking, these records have to be searched in person and not over the telephone. A search of these records is done by name and/or by address. A name search will allow you to review all of the property owned by subjects with the same name(s). An address search will provide you with the owner of the property in question. If the owner of the property has a different mailing address (also listed), this probably indicates that the owner lives elsewhere and rents the property. Contact with the owner of the house using a pre-text form of questioning (discussed later in the book) may allow you to determine the actual tenant. A search of these records is generally free of charge unless copies are requested.

The "Deed Records" are usually compiled with other records that are listed in the same listings and indexes. For instance, the grantor/grantee records (advise who sold/bought property), the power of attorney records (giving relatives or attorneys power to conduct business for you), tax liens, garnishments, child support, guardianship records, and other information are often listed in this index with abbreviations indicating the type of record.

The county's Tax Records may provide useful information and are obtained through the tax office generally located in or near the courthouse. These records can be searched by name and indicate the taxes owed on property for the year. Although the information in the tax records is often times the same as the appraisal district, the mailing address may be different to insure that the owner of the property gets their tax bill. In addition, even though a person may own a business, they may or may not own the place where they operate the business, and are still required to pay taxes on the equipment they own. A mailing address may therefore be listed, and taxes on equipment may provide a listing even though they don't own any property.

The county Assumed Name Records are generally located in the county clerks office in the courthouse and are free to review. These records are filed whenever an individual opens a business or changes their name. A search is conducted by name and if a listing is found, provides the home address and the business addresses. In addition, if there are partners or other owners, these subjects are listed along with their addresses. If the addresses for the subject you are looking for are addresses that you already have, you may consider contacting the other owners using a suitable pre-text form (discussed later in the book).

The county's marriage records are located in the county clerk's office and are usually free to the public to view. The information is checked by searching the person's name. If the person is a female, you will normally need to know their maiden name and/or a former married name to be successful in the

DEED OF GIFT

THE STATE OF TEXAS

KNOW ALL MEN BY THESE PRESENTS:

COUNTY OF LAVACA

That we, David Preston and wife, Janet Preston, of the County of Lavaca, State of Texas, for and in consideration of the love and affection which we have and bear unto and toward our children, John Preston, Sally Preston, and Carl Preston; HAVE GIVEN, GRANTED, AND CONVEYED and by these presents DO GIVE, GRANT, AND CONVEY, in equal shares, unto the said John Preston of Harris County, Texas; Sally Preston of Montgomery County, Texas; and Carl Preston of Harris County, Texas, as a part of their separate estates, an undivided ten per cent (10%) interest in the aggregate in and to the following described tracts of land, subject to the hereinafter set out exceptions and reservations, such tracts of land being described as follows, to wit:

FIRST TRACT:

923.21 acres of land situated in Lavaca County, Texas, a part of the A. Burnhill Survey, Abstract No. 291, A. G. Roberts Heirs Survey, Abstract No. 21, W. G. L. Folles Abstract No. 23, S. T. Folles Survey, and more particularly described by metes and bounds as follows:

BEGINNING at an iron pipe for the Northeast corner of a 1.0 acre tract described in the Deed from the First Baptist Church, to John B. Jones, Jr., Ease line of the A. Marshall Survey, Abstract No. 229, West line of the B. R. Roberts Heirs Survey, Abstract No. 21, an upper Southeast corner of the Alvin J. Marshill 121.32 acre tract of land, same being an inside corner of the herein described tract;

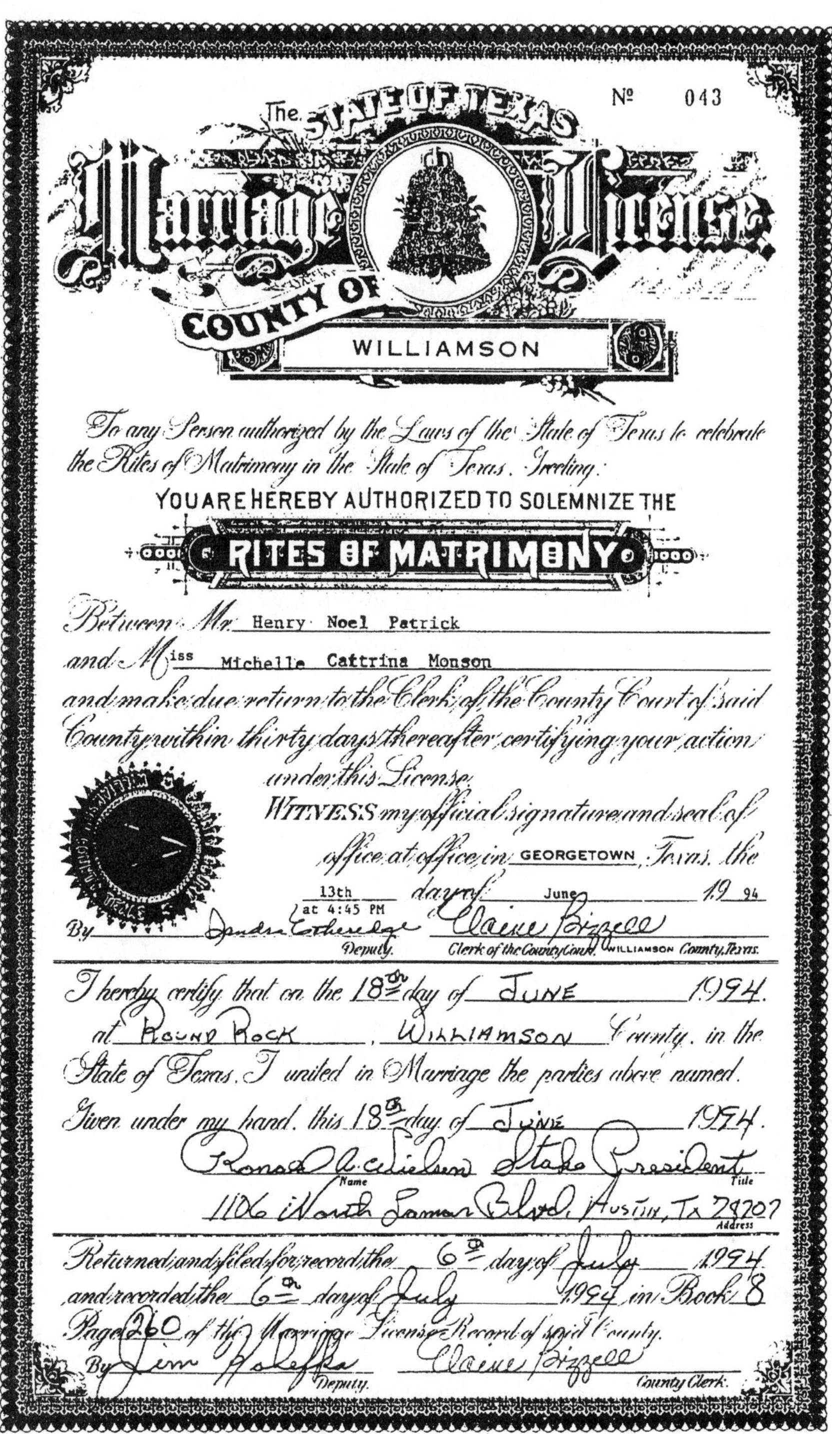

№ 043

The State of Texas
Marriage License
County of WILLIAMSON

To any Person authorized by the Laws of the State of Texas to celebrate the Rites of Matrimony in the State of Texas, Greeting:

YOU ARE HEREBY AUTHORIZED TO SOLEMNIZE THE

RITES OF MATRIMONY

Between Mr. Henry Noel Patrick
and Miss Michelle Cattrina Monson
and make due return to the Clerk of the County Court of said County within thirty days thereafter certifying your action under this License.

WITNESS my official signature and seal of office at office in GEORGETOWN, Texas, the 13th day of June 1994
at 4:45 PM

By Sandra Etheredge Deputy. Elaine Bizzell Clerk of the County Court, WILLIAMSON County, Texas.

I hereby certify that on the 18th day of JUNE 1994, at ROUND ROCK, WILLIAMSON County, in the State of Texas, I united in Marriage the parties above named.

Given under my hand, this 18th day of JUNE 1994.

Ronald A. Nielsen Name Stake President Title
1106 North Lamar Blvd, Austin, Tx 78707 Address

Returned and filed for record the 6th day of July 1994 and recorded the 6th day of July 1994 in Book 8 Page 260 of the Marriage License Record of said County.

By Jim Holeffka Deputy. Elaine Bizzell County Clerk.

HART GRAPHICS, AUSTIN

search. Once a match is found, the address, date of birth, driver's license number, and the social security number will be listed. In addition, the date of marriage, place of marriage, pastor and additional information will be listed upon reviewing the original document. The records are a good source of essential information that can confirm or provide personal information about the subject.

The Municipal Court Records may or may not be open to the public, depending on the policy of your city. A search by name will reveal any tickets issued to the subject. You should be able to review the actual tickets and persistence may be needed to accomplish this. A review of the ticket will provide the reason for the ticket, the location in which they were given the ticket, the person's address, date of birth, the vehicle and license plate numbers, their drivers license number, and sometimes their employer and their social security number.

A Police Department Survey can often be done in the larger cities and requires a fee (usually $5.00 to $25.00). This can be done by calling the police department and confirming that they provide the service, as well as the cost. You can then mail the request and money or do so in person. A survey can be done by name and/or address. You typically have to specify which year(s) that are to be searched. The department may charge a separate fee per year and only the most current may be necessary for locating someone. A survey will provide you with every police call made associated with the subject's name or associated with the address in question. You will be able to identify the date of birth, date and time of the call, location, reason for the call, officers involved, and additional information. This information may be useful or you may contact the officers or the complainant using a pre-text form of questioning (discussed later in the book). This type of search may be done through the Sheriff's Department and/or nearby local suburb police departments.

The Bankruptcy Court Records are located in the Federal building and are typically divided by geographic area of the state. (Ex: The Western District of the Federal Bankruptcy Court handles San Antonio and surrounding areas). A search of these records can usually be done by a phone call. The message will guide you through the system and you use the telephone key pad to punch in the name you wish to search. If a match is found, you will be told the case number, dates involved, the parties involved, and their attorneys. You can then go to their office and personally review the file. The information includes personal information on the subject, debts, amounts, employers, and an abundance of other useful information.

The Secretary of State records provide information on companies which incorporated in that state. The Secretary of State's office can be reached by calling directory assistance in the state's capitol city for that state (Ex: Austin is the capitol of Texas). Ask the clerk for any information concerning the name in question. Some state records can only be accessed by the company's name, while others can do it by the owner's name. The records can tell you when the company incorporated, their "charter number", their business address, and any other companies involved in the ownership of the company. The owner's names and addresses, the officers, and the registered agent can also be identified.

The State Comptroller's Records are also accessed free of charge by telephone and are located in the state capitol of the state. The Comptroller's office regulates sales tax which each company has to pay the state. A search can be done by the individual's names or the company's names. These records will tell you if the subject is paying taxes due to owning a company, a franchise, having an oil or gas well, hotel, mining operations, truck company, or has inherited any money or property. The names and addresses of the owners, officers, and the registered agent can be identified along with other useful information.

If you learn of a person's former high school(s) or university attendance, you may pay attention to the years since their graduation to determine if it is time for an upcoming class reunion. If so, you can contact the school and determine who is organizing the reunion and from there, determine any current information on the subject. As a last resort, you may be able to attend the reunion and locate the subject.

Another source of daily information is the newspapers. By simply paying attention to photographs and daily police call listings (where published) you may stumble across the subject or a relative. I can remember 4-5 cases where I found a person who was involved in a car accident or was listed in the daily police "blotter" in the newspaper. If nothing else, it at least tells you that the subject has not skipped town.

Depending on the subject's line of business, you may be able to contact the Visitor's Bureau in larger cities or the Chamber of Commerce to determine the list of upcoming conventions, dates, and persons responsible for the organization. Through this, you may be able to determine if your subject is listed as a vender scheduled to have a display, a member of a club or company, and additional facts.

The Department of Vital Statistics is a good place to check birth and death records. The offices are generally headquartered in the capitol city of the state and often have branch offices in larger cities. You can confirm the person's legal information, relatives, and other useful facts. The birth certificate will also have the parent's place of birth and will be an asset, as often times there are still relatives in that area. If searching for a death certificate with very little information, request a name search over a period of several years. If the subject is still alive, but is unable to be found, check for relatives who may have recently passed away. The funeral home will be listed on the certificate and it may be a good source of information to determine who made the arrangements, etc.

The Medical Examiner's office may be an additional source of finding relatives who have passed away and had an autopsy performed. In some areas this information is open to the public. The reports will list the names, addresses, and telephone numbers of relatives.

The State Department of Parks and Wildlife/Game Warden should be contacted to determine if the subject has a hunting or fishing license. If the person is truly trying to hide, they may go into camping and fishing areas. The department's records can indicate where the license was issued and this may be near to the location of the subject. It may also give a different address for the person.

A search of the State's Department of Aviation FAA should be considered to determine if the subject has a plane registered to them. If so, the records can indicate where the airplane is sheltered. From this, you may be able to locate the subject's flight plans.

Once these records are researched, your next step depends on the information you just obtained. If you did not locate the subject through these searches, you should conduct the same searches in the counties that surround the county in which the subject was last known to be. If this still does not provide the desired results, check the same records in the largest cities close to you. Most people who try to hide, commonly seek large cities which enable them to hide more easily. When all of these sources have been exhausted, you may have to initiate other alternatives (discussed later in this book).

However, one such alternative would be to contact a PI and have them conduct a name search in a particular area (Ex: city or state). The information provided will include all of the subjects in the area searched who have the same or similar names, their addresses, and their telephone numbers. The PI usually has access to computer programs that are legal to have, but are not accessible to the public. The author of this information will gladly provide the material for a fee of $19.95 and can be done by calling (210) 493-3366 or by writing to Kelmar and Associates Investigations, 11840 Wurzbach, San Antonio, TX. 78230.

SECURITY AGREEMENT

DATE March 9 19 89

SSN -66-8065

DEBTOR	RODNEY C.	SECURED PARTY	BAY CITY BANK & TRUST CO.
BUSINESS OR RESIDENCE ADDRESS	P.O. Box 108	ADDRESS	1919 7TH STREET, P.O. BOX 471
CITY, STATE & ZIP CODE	Rockport, Texas 78382	CITY, STATE & ZIP CODE	BAY CITY, TEXAS 77414

1. Security Interest and Collateral. To secure the payment and performance of each and every debt, liability and obligation of every type and description which Debtor may now or at any time hereafter owe to Secured Party (whether such debt, liability or obligation now exists or is hereafter created or incurred, and whether it is or may be direct or indirect, due or to become due, absolute or contingent, primary or secondary, liquidated or unliquidated, or joint, several or joint and several; all such debts, liabilities and obligations being herein collectively referred to as the "Obligations"), Debtor hereby grants Secured Party a security interest (herein called the "Security Interest") in the following property (herein called the "Collateral") (check applicable boxes and complete information):

(a) INVENTORY:
XX All inventory of Debtor, whether now owned or hereafter acquired and wherever located;

(b) EQUIPMENT, FARM PRODUCTS AND CONSUMER GOODS:
XX All equipment of Debtor, whether now owned or hereafter acquired, including but not limited to all present and future machinery, vehicles, furniture, fixtures, manufacturing equipment, farm machinery and equipment, shop equipment, office and recordkeeping equipment, parts and tools, and the goods described in any equipment schedule or list herewith or hereafter furnished to Secured Party by Debtor (but no such schedule or list need be furnished in order for the security interest granted herein to be valid as to all of Debtor's equipment).

XX All farm products of Debtor, whether now owned or hereafter acquired, including but not limited to (i) all poultry and livestock and their young, products thereof and produce thereof, (ii) all crops, whether annual or perennial, and the products thereof, and (iii) all feed, seed, fertilizer, medicines and other supplies used or produced by Debtor in farming operations. The real estate concerned with the above described crops growing or to be grown is:

FARM PRODUCTS-As per attached "Exhibit A", Page 1
FARM EQUIPMENT-As per attached "Exhibit A", Page 1

and the name of the record owner is: ____________________

☐ The following goods or types of goods: ____________________

(c) ACCOUNTS AND OTHER RIGHTS TO PAYMENT:
XX Each and every right of Debtor to the payment of money, whether such right to payment now exists or hereafter arises, whether such right to payment arises out of a sale, lease or other disposition of goods or other property by Debtor, out of a rendering of services by Debtor, out of a loan by Debtor, out of the overpayment of taxes or other liabilities of Debtor, or otherwise arises under any contract or agreement, whether such right to payment is or is not already earned by performance, and howsoever such right to payment may be evidenced, together with all other rights and interests (including all liens and security interests) which Debtor may at any time have by law or agreement against any account debtor or other obligor obligated to make any such payment or against any of the property of such account debtor or other obligor; all including but not limited to all present and future debt instruments, chattel papers, accounts, and loans and obligations receivable.

☐ ____________________

(d) GENERAL INTANGIBLES:
☐ All general intangibles of Debtor, whether now owned or hereafter acquired, including, but not limited to, applications for patents, patents, copyrights, trademarks, trade secrets, good will, tradenames, customer lists, permits and franchises, the right to use Debtor's name, and tax refunds.

gether with all substitutions and replacements for and products of any of the foregoing property not constituting consumer goods and together with proceeds of ny and all of the foregoing property and, in the case of all tangible Collateral, together with all accessions and, except in the case of consumer goods, together ith (i) all accessories, attachments, parts, equipment and repairs now or hereafter attached or affixed to or used in connection with any such goods, and (ii) all arehouse receipts, bills of lading and other documents of title now or hereafter covering such goods.

. Representations, Warranties and Agreements. Debtor represents, warrants and agrees that:

(a) Debtor is ☒ an individual, ☐ a partnership, ☐ a corporation and, if Debtor is an individual, the Debtor's residence is at the address of Debtor shown at the beginning of this Agreement.

(b) The Collateral will be used primarily for ☐ personal, family or household purposes ☒ farming operations; ☐ business purposes.

(c) ☐ If any part or all of the tangible Collateral will become so related to particular real estate as to become a fixture, the real estate concerned is: ____________________

and the name of the record owner is: ____________________

(d) Debtor's chief executive office is located at ____________________
or, if left blank, at the address of Debtor shown at the beginning of this Agreement.

3243

STATE OF TEXAS I

COUNTY OF WEBB I

Before me, the undersigned authority, on this day personally appeared CARLOS MARTIN known to me to be the person who subscribed his/her name below, who, after having first been duly sworn by me, on oath deposes and says:

That , CARLOS MARTIN , IS NOT one and the same person as CARLOS H. MARTIN AND CARLOS MARTIN , ET AL, named in a VARIOUS STATE TAX LIENS AND ONE FEDERAL TAX LIEN styled (SEE ATTACHED EXHIBIT "A") vs __________,

__________, __________,

__________, dated __________,

and recorded in Vol. _____, page(s) _____ of the __________

County __________.

Further affiant sayeth not.

VOL 107 PAGE 63

[signature]
CARLOS MARTIN

Subscribed and sworn to by the said CARL MARTIN this 14th day of SEPTEMBER, 1984.

(L.S.)

FILED: 9-18-84 AT 3:20 P.M.
HENRY FLORES
COUNTY CLERK, WEBB COUNTY, TEXAS

[signature]
Notary Public in and for the State of Texas
GLORIA E. ESCOBEDO
Printed Name of Notary
My Commission expires: 9-3-88.

STATE OF TEXAS I

COUNTY OF WEBB I

This instrument was acknowledged this [illegible] day of [illegible], 198[illegible]

[signature]
Notary Public in and for the State of Texas

GLOR[illegible] ESCOBEDO
Printed Name of Notary
My Commission expires: 9-3-88.

(L.S.)

CHAPTER THREE

Locating Minors

The ability to locate a child or a teenager requires a different approach because more than likely, they will not be listed in any of the records we have discussed. This type of individual has not had ample time to become involved in the "system", has not established credit, and probably has lived with a parental figure. Therefore, the whole technique of "locating" a person such as this requires ingenuity.

The most common reason for a "missing person" in this age group is that the individual believes that the grass is greener on the other side. In this situation, the person has usually developed an anti-authority attitude and believes that they are self-sufficient. These individuals typically become run-aways who soon discover the reality of growing up. Unfortunately, pride becomes a major obstacle in the person admitting that they were wrong and returning home.

Another reason for a missing person in this category is due to abduction. Abduction is commonly thought of as a mentally ill person abducting children. However, the truth is that this is an extremely small percentage of missing persons. The media has paid more attention to this in recent years which has increased the public's awareness of this. However, the most common "abduction" is usually associated with an ex-spouse abducting the child from the legal guardian. In a lot of these cases, the ex-spouse can almost anticipate this due to the nature of their former spouse. Unfortunately, the law does not give much protection until an attempted abduction is made. A system of precautions can be initiated which will serve to deter these types of situations. These include contacting the school, teachers, daycare workers, neighbors, doctors, and others who have frequent contact with the child. Each of these subjects need to be made aware of the concerns so that extra care is provided to insure the child's safety while in their care. The parent should consider investing in a pager so that immediate communication concerning any irregularity or concern can immediately be discussed.

There are other reasons for a person in this category being listed as "missing". These may include the child becoming sick or injured causing them to be in the care of a medical facility. The child may have gone into some nearby woods to play and lost their sense of direction. Regardless of the reason for the person being listed as "missing", the first 72 hours after the person is determined to be missing is critical.

First, do the obvious. Contact the police department and initiate a report with their office. Be sure to contact the local police department, the sheriff's department, and the Department of Public Safety. Unfortunately, due to their work load, information passed between these agencies is sometimes over-looked. Make sure that they are all made aware of the situation by contacting them individually.

Next, stop and analyze the information that you have at hand. Check the missing person's room to see if anything important to them is missing. Determine if their piggy-bank is empty because any pre-determined run-away plan would involve taking money and supplies. Check your own wallets to see if any of your credit cards are gone. The person may have thought that you would not miss only one card. If you find a card missing, notify the credit card agency of your situation. With their cooperation, you may be able to track the person's movements by the purchases made. If you have any coin collections or other hidden valuables, check to see if they are missing as the individual may attempt to use or sell this for cash. Check the clothes that are in the person's closet, especially those the person is fond of. Determine if a coat, blanket, pillow, teddy-bear, flashlight, bicycle, camping equipment, or other similar items are gone.

While checking the missing items around the house, look for any guns that may have been hidden in the house. The person may have taken this for protection or to sell. If there is a pet which the person was close to, determine if it is present. If the pet is a dog, this may be a good source to assist in locating the person. Have someone canvass the area and call out for the dog. Hopefully, the pet will respond and provide the person's location. If you have a computer at home, check for any letters you do not recognize. The person may have used the computer to write to another party where they intended to go. Double check any messages on the answering machine for any clues or useful information. If your telephone has the automatic call back feature, use this to see where the last call was made. Take time to reflect on any statements or conversations with the person which may give you insight into the situation.

Depending on the age of the person, all or some of the following information may apply. Once you have evaluated the house and any items which may have been taken, you should have a better understanding as to whether or not the person had a pre-conceived run-away plan. Contact the neighbors and any friends of the subject. Find out when they last talked to the missing person, where they talked to them, what they were wearing, who was with them, what their attitude was like, and if they made any comments about where they were headed. If the friend is aware that the subject ran-away, they probably will try to cover for them. Always check with the parents of these subjects as they may have overheard conversations. I am aware of one case in which the parents were hiding the run-away because they thought child abuse had been occurring. Actually, that was not the case, but the run-away and his friend made the parents believe that the abuse had occurred. I remember another case in which the run-away was being let into the friend's bedroom window at night and out again in the morning before anyone knew they were there. Make sure that the neighbors and parents know the entire situation so that they can correctly monitor their own child. While talking with the missing person's friends, ask them about other friends, girlfriends/boyfriends, club houses or "safe-houses", any recent fights or arguments, or anyone unusual who they may have been seen with including service/repair personnel, taxi cabs, etc. Hopefully, these contacts will provide useful information to follow up on.

Next, check the hang-outs where people of their age group go. Malls are a good place to search. Be sure to check with the mall security officers who probably will recognize the subject if they hang around the mall. Locate a recent photograph of the missing person, make copies, and leave them with the people you talk to (along with your telephone number and/or pager number). Malls have become the place for teenagers to socialize and would therefore be a good place to start.

Check places like video arcades, restaurants that kids frequent, parks, theaters, skating rinks, and other hang-outs. Check with the taxi cab companies, bus lines, airlines, truck stops, or other methods the party may be using to leave the area. Do not assume that these places will be checked by the police. Unfortunately, each department has different guidelines on the amount of time required to pass before they list the person as missing. Once they agree to list them as missing, they enter the person's name into the nation-wide computer system which links all law enforcement agencies together. They will usually make the patrol units aware of the situation in case they come into contact with the subject. However, in the majority of the cases, that is the extent of the police departments involvement and resources.

Check with the local hospitals and clinics to determine if the person is in their care. Be sure to ask about any "John Doe's or Jane Doe's" that they have in their facility. If the person was brought in without any identification, they are listed as a John Doe or Jane Doe until identification is made.

Contact the local police departments and find out if they have a gang unit or juvenile division. Talk with these officers to see if they have come into contact with the person. Sometimes the gang unit may know the subject by a name given to them by the gang, but not by their real name. Determine the extent of gang activity in that area, where their hang-outs are, and what their "colors" are. The gang's colors are usually some type of clothing and/or tattoo that immediately identifies them to other gang members. Determine whether or not the missing person has been seen wearing any of these colors. Also contact the juvenile court judges to determine whether or not they know the subject in question. They may have been in court with a friend and not actually called before the judge. A check with juvenile detention centers may be a good idea to see if a person has been placed there until the person became sober or coherent after drug use.

Direct contact with teachers, counselors, janitors, coaches, cafeteria personnel and other school related figures should be made. These people may be able to tell you who they associated with, information over-heard in conversations, or other pertinent information. A check with the pastor of your church, boy-scout leaders, music, karate or other extra-curricular activities should also be conducted. Determine if any of these people ever saw the subject with a pager. People who become entangled with drugs often use pagers to carry-out their distribution.

If the subject had any bank account, contact the bank to see if the accounts are still open and any recent activity with the account. Check your own telephone bills for numbers you do not recognize. Review the recent credit card statements for purchases you are not aware of.

Although most record searches will not apply in this situation, contact the local utility departments and request that a name search be done on the subject. Hopefully, if the person set up an apartment and the rent does not include utilities, you may find the person this way. Check with directory assistance to see if the person has recently had a telephone turned on in their name or in the name of close friends. Even though their friends may still be at home, they may use the friend's name to get services to continue to hide. It may be wise to check with the military recruiters in your area to determine if the subject enlisted and did not tell you out of fear of disapproval. If you reside near a U.S. border crossing, contact the check-points and alert the officials of your situation. If the person is old enough to drive and has been gone for sometime, check with the state (usually the Department of Public Safety) to see if the subject's driver's license has been forfeited to another state. If a person moves out of state, they have to relinquish their driver's license before obtaining one in the new state. The records will indicate where the subject obtained a new license. You should then contact that state and determine the current address. If the person left with camping or hunting equipment, contact the Department of Parks and Wildlife so that they can alert their officers to watch for the subject.

Locating missing persons of this nature presents a totally different approach, as demonstrated. The key to success is initiating the search quickly and analyzing all of the bits of information which will hopefully present the entire picture.

If these tools do not provide the necessary information in which to locate the subject, consider searches outlined in Chapter Two, "Locating People".

CHAPTER FOUR

LOCATING INSURANCE COVERAGE

PI's often get contacted to assist in determining whether an individual has insurance. The typical need for this arises from an automobile accident where the other party was at fault but does not appear to have insurance. The other common need occurs when some type of injury or incident occurs on a piece of property in which the owner refuses to identify their insurance carrier.

First of all, these are some of the harder investigations because there is not one central or common source which lists a person's insurance company. It is not uncommon to randomly telephone the larger insurance companies and determine through an appropriate pre-text form of questioning (discussed later in the book) whether or not the subject has insurance through their particular company.

The Pauper? I became involved in a case when an insurance company contacted me and requested a hidden assets investigation. The subject of the investigation was an elderly man in his

70's who was driving an older model truck and had collided with their insured's vehicle. The subject apparently did not have insurance and my client was therefore faced with paying the damages and medical bills for their insured. The client requested that I determine if the subject did have insurance and if he had any assets free of liens which they could place a lien against. The client was skeptical from the beginning and did not anticipate finding any useful information. What I found was an elderly man who had almost 1 million dollars worth of land, without liens attached, oil wells producing revenue on some of the land, a large herd of cattle, and insurance. By checking the county deed records, I discovered the majority of the land. I learned of more property through the Appraisal District records and the Tax Records and learned of the cattle by checking the county's "brand" books which detail what brands ranchers use on their livestock. I then requested a name search for any accidents or incidents involving the subject for the past 5 years through the Department of Public Safety and the local police department. I found several other accident reports which listed the subject's insurance company. A few quick calls to the insurance company, and I had confirmed that the coverage was still current. Needless to say, I had one happy client and all of the information was learned through the methods described in this book.

To determine the insurance on a house or piece of property, there are several methods to obtain this goal. First, the County's Appraisal District Records can be researched free of charge and are usually located near or in the courthouse. A search by the owner's name or the address itself can be conducted. Most of the time, the mortgage company, bank, or other lienholder is listed. Once you have this information, you can call the mortgage company and utilizing a pre-text form of questioning, determine the insurance carrier. The mortgage company or bank will require that the property be insured to protect their loan or investment.

If the Appraisal District office does not give you the mortgage company, conduct a search through the County's Deed Records. This is usually located in the courthouse and is free of charge. A search by name will provide a listing of all properties owned by the subject, the legal description of the property, and the mortgage company. Contact with the mortgage company can then be made utilizing a proper pre-text form to determine the insurance carrier.

The County's Tax Records is a third source of determining the mortgage company. The appraisal district records, the county's deed records and the county tax records all have access to the mortgage company, however, most of the time only one of the three has the information included. A search by name or address can also be conducted through their records free of charge. Once the mortgage company is obtained, you can use the appropriate pre-text form of questioning to determine the insurance carrier.

To determine the insurance carrier on a vehicle, it is necessary to locate the lienholder first. The lienholder requires that the owner of a vehicle maintain insurance on the vehicle until the loan is paid off. The first way to determine this is to obtain a copy of the police department accident report which is completed on every accident the police department handles, and usually cost $1.00 to $5.00. On the police department's report is a space for the person's insurance company. Assuming that this has been done and there is no information listed for this, contact the State's Department of Transportation and Public Highways located in the capitol city of your state. Some states have a telephone number that you can call and by giving them the license plate number, they will provide you with the owner's name, address, vehicle information, and the lienholder. If your state does not have a telephone service dedicated to the public, you will have to write and request the information. It is not uncommon for the department to charge a $2.00 to $10.00 fee for this service. If the State Department of Transportation will not provide this information in your state, some PI's will run the license plate for you for a nominal fee. Kelmar and Associates will be happy to provide this information by calling (210) 493-3366.

If you suspect that a person may have a life insurance policy, but don't know where (Ex: relative dies abruptly), you may want to contact the American Council of Life Insurance, ATTN: Policy Search, at 1001 Pennsylvania Avenue, N. W., Washington, D. C. 20004.

The Department of Veterans Affairs is also a source to check to determine if there are any unclaimed benefits due to veterans and their families. You can call 1-800-829-1040 to initiate the search.

The Office of Personnel Management oversees benefits due to former Federal employees and their spouses. They currently have several million in unclaimed benefits. To search, write to the office at the "Retirement Operations Center", Boyers, PA. 16017.

Driver's License Offices

ALABAMA
Drivers License Division
State of Alabama
P. O. Box 1471
Montgomery, Alabama 36192

ALASKA
Drivers License Division
State of Alaska
P. O. Box 20020
Juneau, Alaska 99802

ARIZONA
Drivers License Division
State of Arizona
P. O. Box 2100
Phoenix, Arizona 85001

ARKANSAS
Drivers License Division
P. O. Box 1272
Little Rock, Arkansas 72203

CALIFORNIA
Drivers License Division
State of California
P. O. Box 944231
Sacramento, California 94244

COLORADO
Drivers License Division
State of Colorado
140 W. 6th Ave.
Denver, Colorado 80204

CONNECTICUT
Drivers License Division
State of Connecticut
60 State Street
Wethersfield, Connecticut 06109

DELAWARE
Drivers License Division
State of Delaware
P. O. Box 698
Dover, Delaware 19903

DISTRICT OF COLUMBIA
Drivers License Division
District of Columbia
301 C Street, N.W.
Washington, D. C. 20001

FLORIDA
Drivers License Division
State of Florida
Neil Kirkman Building
Tallahassee, Florida 32399

GEORGIA
Drivers License Division
State of Georgia
P. O. Box 1456
Atlanta, Georgia 30371

HAWAII
Drivers License Division
State of Hawaii
530 S. King St.
Honolulu, Hawaii 96813

IDAHO
Drivers License Division
State of Idaho
P. O. Box 7129
Boise, Idaho 83707

ILLINOIS
Drivers License Division
State of Illinois
2701 S. Dirksen Parkway
Springfield, Illinois 62723

INDIANA
Drivers License Division
State of Indiana
State Office Building
Indianapolis, Indiana 46204

IOWA
Drivers License Division
State of Iowa
100 Euclid Ave.
Des Moines, Iowa 50306

KANSAS
Drivers License Division
State of Kansas
Docking Office Building
Topeka, Kansas 66626

KENTUCKY
Drivers License Division
State of Kentucky
State Office Building
Frankfort, Kentucky 40622

LOUISIANA
Drivers License Division
State of Louisiana
P. O. Box 64886
Baton Rouge, Louisiana 70896

MAINE
Drivers License Division
State of Maine
State House, Room 29
Augusta, Maine 04333

MARYLAND
Drivers License Division
State of Maryland
6601 Ritchie Highway, N.E.
Room 211
Glen Burnie, Maryland 21062

MASSACHUSETTS
Drivers License Division
Commonwealth of Massachusetts
100 Nashua St.
Boston, Massachusetts 02114

MICHIGAN
Drivers License Division
State of Michigan
7064 Crowner Dr.
Lansing, Michigan 48918

MINNESOTA
Drivers License Division
State of Minnesota
Transportation Building, Room 108
Saint Paul, Minnesota 55155

MISSISSIPPI
Drivers License Division
State of Mississippi
P.O. Box 958
Jackson, Mississippi 39205

MISSOURI
Drivers License Division
State of Missouri
P.O. Box 200
Jefferson City, Missouri 65105

MONTANA
Drivers License Division
State of Montana
303 North Roberts
Helena, Montana 59620

NEBRASKA
Drivers License Division
State of Nebraska
301 Centennial Mall South
Lincoln, Nebraska 68509

NEVADA
Drivers License Division
State of Nevada
555 Wright Way
Carson City, Nevada 89711

NEW HAMPSHIRE
Drivers License Division
State of New Hampshire
10 Hazen Dr.
Concord, New Hampshire 03305

NEW JERSEY
Drivers License Division
State of New Jersey
25 South Montgomery St.
Trenton, New Jersey 08666

NEW MEXICO
Drivers License Division
State of New Mexico
P.O. Box 1028
Santa Fe, New Mexico 87504

NEW YORK
Drivers License Division
State of New York
Empire State Plaza
Albany, New York 12228

NORTH CAROLINA
Drivers License Division
State of North Carolina
1100 New Bern Ave.
Raleigh, North Carolina 27697

NORTH DAKOTA
Drivers License Division
State of North Dakota
Capitol Grounds
Bismarck, North Dakota 58505

OHIO
Drivers License Division
State of Ohio
P.O. Box 7167
Columbus, Ohio 43266

OKLAHOMA
Drivers License Division
State of Oklahoma
P.O. Box 11415
Oklahoma City, Oklahoma 73136

OREGON
Drivers License Division
State of Oregon
1905 Lana Ave., N.E.
Salem, Oregon 97314

PENNSYLVANIA
Drivers License Division
State of Pennsylvania
P.O. Box 8695
Harrisburg, Pennsylvania 17105

PUERTO RICO
Drivers License Division
Commonwealth of Puerto Rico
P.O. Box 41243
Santurce, Puerto Rico 00940

RHODE ISLAND
Drivers License Division
State of Rhode Island
345 Harris Ave.
Providence, Rhode Island 02909

SOUTH CAROLINA
Drivers License Division
State of South Carolina
P.O. Box 1498
Columbia, South Carolina 29216

SOUTH DAKOTA
Drivers License Division
State of South Dakota
118 W. Capitol Ave.
Pierre, South Dakota 57501

TENNESSEE
Drivers License Division
State of Tennessee
P.O. Box 945
Nashville, Tennessee 37202

TEXAS
Drivers License Division
State of Texas
P.O. Box 4087
Austin, Texas 78773

UTAH
Drivers License Division
State of Utah
1095 Motor Ave.
Salt Lake City, Utah 84116

VERMONT
Drivers License Division
State of Vermont
120 State Street
Montpelier, Vermont 05603

VIRGINIA
Drivers License Division
State of Virginia
2300 W. Broad St.
Richmond, Virginia 23269

WASHINGTON
Drivers License Division
State of Washington
211 12th Ave., S.E.
Olympia, Washington 98504

WEST VIRGINIA
Drivers License Division
State of West Virginia
1800 Washington St., East
Charleston, West Virginia 25317

WISCONSIN
Drivers License Division
State of Wisconsin
P.O. Box 7918
Madison, Wisconsin 53707

WYOMING
Drivers License Division
State of Wyoming
122 W. 25th St.
Cheyenne, Wyoming 82002

CHAPTER FIVE

LEGITIMATE CREDENTIALS?

PI's are commonly asked to assist an employer in determining whether a person's credentials are legitimate. In addition, individuals often want to know if their doctor, security guard, or insurance agent actually has the necessary credentials.

I was retained to check the general background of my client's potential spouse. According my client, she had just received a proposal of marriage from a man she had only known for approximately six months. Her potential spouse was allegedly a millionaire, had never been married, owned several businesses, and was a Rhodes Scholar. After meeting with the client for the first time and deciding to accept the case, the client called the office the next day. She was apparently being followed as her fiance had questioned her about going to see a PI. During the course of the investigation, the client was always paged so that a pay phone could be used, as well as a code name because she believed her telephone was being tapped. During the record checks conducted, I determined that the subject had

3. Date, Time, Number and Filing Office: (Filing Officer's Use Only)

SECY OF TEXAS
JUN 25 90 0183
FILED [illegible] AM

A

1. Debtor(s) Name and Mailing Address: (Do not abbreviate)

UTURO FARMS, INC.
P.O. Box 1087
Rockport, Texas 78382
Tx. I.D.#76-0205 7

Microfilm Index Number: (Filing Officer's Use Only)

2. Secured Party(ies) Name and Mailing Address:

BAY CITY BANK AND TRUST COMPANY
P.O. Box 471
Bay City, Tx. 77404-0471

4. Assignee Name and Mailing Address:

5. This Financing Statement covers the following types (or items) of property.
(WARNING: If collateral is crops, fixtures, timber or minerals, read instructions on back.)

FARM PRODUCTS-AS per attached Security Agreement & "Exhibit A", Page 1

ASSIGNMENT USDA REGULATIONS AND/OR PAYMENTS-As per attached Security Agreement & "Exhibit A", Page 1

2nd LIEN DEED OF TRUST-As per attached Security Agreement & "Exhibit A", Page 1

Check only if applicable

[XX] Products of collateral are also covered.

[ ] This Financing Statement is to be filed for record in the real estate records. Number of additional sheets presented ______

6. This Financing Statement is signed by the Secured Party instead of the Debtor to perfect a security interest in collateral

Check appropriate box

[ ] already subject to a security interest in another jurisdiction when it was brought into this state, or when the debtor's location was changed to this state, or
[ ] already subject to a financing statement filed in another county, or
[ ] which is proceeds of the original collateral described above in which a security interest was perfected, or
[ ] as to which the filing has lapsed, or
[ ] acquired after a change of name, identity or corporate structure of the debtor.

UTURO FARMS, INC.
(Charles Schindle , President)

Use whichever signature line is applicable

BAY CITY BANK AND TRUST COMPANY
(Bill Humphrey, Jr., Exec. Vice Pres

By Charles Schindle Pres.
Signature(s) of Debtor(s)

By [signature]
Signature(s) of Secured Party(ies)

This Financing Statement is presented to a Filing Officer for filing pursuant to the Uniform Commercial Code

(1) Filing Officer Copy—Numerical

STANDARD FORM—FORM UCC-1 (Rev. 0-1-87) © 1985 OFFICE OF THE SECRETARY OF STATE OF TEXAS been married, was just recently divorced, and had assaulted his ex-wife. The subject had a large amount of civil lawsuits filed against him and he was currently under indictment by the FBI. According to the records, the subject's father owned the business, which included an airplane charter service. The FBI believed the airplane service was being used as a front for illegal activity. A check of the subject's educational background revealed he had attended college, but not the "Ivy League" school he had indicated, and he was not a Rhodes Scholar.

If the person is a professional who owns a company or provides a service, contact the Better Business Bureau to determine whether or not the person or company has any complaints filed against them. Secondly, contact the State's Attorney General's Office who usually has offices in the larger cities and is headquartered in the capitol city of the state. Ask for the complaint/investigative division and they will tell you if the person has any complaints filed against them with their office.

A practice that is becoming more and more common is for an insurance agent to take a person's money and then advise them that they have insurance coverage. However, the agent never turns the money in to the insurance company and there is no coverage when needed. To prevent this from happening, first call the insurance company which the agent represents and confirm that the agent is in good standing and hasn't been suspended. Secondly, contact the State Board of Insurance which is located in the capitol city of the state. They can confirm that the agent is licensed as an insurance agent and is in good standing with the state.

Because there is a need for a large number of security guards, some people with questionable backgrounds are hired by security companies due to the demand for guards. Therefore, no one should assume that a security guard and the security guard company are legitimate. The State Board of Security Guards oversees the licensing of guards and guard companies. This agency is located in the capitol city of the state and will provide information to you free of charge. The agency will confirm that the guard company is licensed, who the owner and manager is, and whether or not they are in good standing. The agency will advise whether or not a person is licensed as a security guard, if they are licensed to carry a gun, how long they have been a security guard, and any complaints against the person.

The State Board of Medical Examiners is located in the capitol city of the state and provides free information to the public. Contact with this agency will confirm that a person is licensed as a doctor in that state, his business address, when he became licensed, and which medical school they graduated from. The agency will also advise you whether or not there are any complaints filed against the doctor and if the doctor has ever been suspended. It is suggested that the registrar's office at the medical school the doctor graduated from be contacted to confirm that they actually attended and graduated from the school. If the school is located in a different state, you should contact that State's Board of Medical Examiners to make sure the doctor didn't move to prevent an attempt to revoke their license. It should be noted that dentists and doctors who are specialists have separate and/or additional State Boards (Ex: State Board of Dentistry) which oversee their actions. These agencies should also be contacted as they will provide the searches free of charge.

When hiring an individual or when attempting to confirm a person's college credentials, contact the registrar's office for the college. They can search by name or social security number and will confirm that the person attended the college, when they graduated, and their major.

In addition to the individual State Boards listed herein, other professionals typically have State Boards which oversee their profession which include some of the following:

1) Aircraft Mechanics
2) Airports
3) Alarm Contractors
4) Alarm Installers
5) Auctioneers
6) Auto Inspectors
7) Auto Wreckers
8) Bankers
9) Barbers
10) Bill Collectors
11) Building Contractors
12) Carpet Cleaners
13) Certified Public Accountants
14) Embalmers
15) Investigators
16) Notary Public
17) Pest Controllers
18) Pharmacists
19) Stock Brokers
20) Veterinarians

All of these boards attempt to regulate their individual professions for the good of all. Therefore, they will have all of the pertinent information concerning the subject, background information, and hopefully current addresses and telephone numbers.

Once these searches are completed, already mentioned in preceding paragraph's, the County's Criminal and Civil Records, the Secretary of State's Office, and the State Comptroller's Office should also be searched to be complete in your investigation.

A check with prior employers should be conducted. Depending on the time requirements for hiring a new employee, you may have to call them. However, a written request with certain pre-determined questions designed for short answers should be used when possible. Regardless of the method, a check list of questions should be developed to ask pertinent questions in a concise manner. The former employer is limited by law in revealing certain information about the person and some will only answer the most basic of questions. You should attempt to verify the person's social security number, date of birth, dates of employment, any disciplinary action taken, information regarding job related injuries, whether or not the person was bonded or had to undergo polygraph or drug testing, and other questions such as these.

Any gaps in the person's employment or education should immediately be addressed. The subject may have been in jail, in a mental hospital, or other situations which you should be aware of. If the person indicates they attempted to start their own business, see if they can supply any indication to support this. A good start would be a copy of their incorporation records, a copy of the assumed name record, a business card, or other documents. Depending on the nature of the job they have applied for, reasons for the failure of the business may reveal that they are not good at marketing, management, or do not possess good people skills.

A check with the State Workman's Compensation Board should be conducted to see if the person has had any employment related injuries in the past. You will probably have to write to the department to receive a response. It is not uncommon for a subject who has had prior workman's compensation injuries to have additional injuries due to the weakening of the body caused by the pre-existing injury. They may be limited in their physical abilities and the doctor may have given them a partial disability rating. The abuse of the worker's compensation system is on the increase and those people who had prior claims may be prime candidates for filing additional claims. If a person is found to have prior claims, you will be notified of the dates, employers, type of injury, doctors, attorneys, insurance carrier, and other useful information. Some states do not provide this information to the public, however, most still do.

A check of the county civil records should be conducted through checking the county clerk's office and the county district clerk's office. Both are located in the courthouse and are free to access. The county civil records are typically the "small claims court" and involve minimum amounts of damages. The district civil records house the cases with higher damages, divorce cases, bad debts, personal injury cases, and other similar cases. A search of these records may reveal lawsuits pertaining to a workmen's compensation injury, auto accident injury, judgement, bad debt, tax lien, or other important material. If a recent divorce or delinquent debt is located, this may suggest that the person is going through a stressful period in their life and you may need to evaluate the person's possible employment in greater detail.

The county criminal records, which are housed in the district court clerk's office and the county clerk's office just like the civil records, should also be checked. You may find that the subject has committed embezzlement in their former employment, has been charged with theft, or may be known for bouncing checks. The subject may have been charged with DWI, public intoxication, drug related offenses, child abuse, or other offenses which should be considered before hiring the subject.

Each job applicant provides a resume which includes different information from the others you receive. Some have a great deal of information, while others have minimal facts available. Because of this diversity, the person should be required to complete a standard employment application that asks the same information of each applicant. This will allow you to compare "apples to apples" to insure that enough material is provided for an appropriate interview and verification of their credentials.

Medical Boards

ALABAMA
Alabama Medical Board
P.O. Box 36101
Montgomery, Alabama 36101

ALASKA
Alaska Medical Board
P.O. Box D
Juneau, Alaska 99811

ARIZONA
Arizona Medical Board
3601 West Camelback Road
Phoenix, Arizona 85015

ARKANSAS
Arkansas Medical Board
P.O. Box 102
Harrisburg, Arkansas 72432

CALIFORNIA
California Medical Board
1426 Howe Avenue
Sacramento, California 95825

COLORADO
Colorado Medical Board
1560 Broadway
Denver, Colorado 80202

CONNECTICUT
Connecticut Medical Board
150 Washington Street
Hartford, Connecticut 06106

DELAWARE
Delaware Medical Board
P.O. Box 1401
Dover, Delaware 19903

DISTRICT OF COLUMBIA
D. C. Medical Board
605 G. Street, Northwest
Washington, D.C. 20001

FLORIDA
Florida Medical Board
1940 North Monroe Street
Tallahassee, Florida 32399

GEORGIA
Georgia Medical Board
166 Pryor Street, Southwest
Atlanta, Georgia 30303

HAWAII
Hawaii Medical Board
P.O. Box 3469
Honolulu, Hawaii 96801

IDAHO
Idaho Medical Board
280 North 8th Street
Boise, Idaho 83720

ILLINOIS
Illinois Medical Board
320 West Washington
Springfield, Illinois 62786

INDIANA
Indiana Medical Board
One American Square
Indianapolis, Indiana 46282

IOWA
Iowa Medical Board
1209 West Court Avenue
Des Moines, Iowa 50319

KANSAS
Kansas Medical Board
235 Southwest Topeka Boulevard
Topeka, Kansas 66603

KENTUCKY
Kentucky Medical Board
400 Sherbon Lane
Louisville, Kentucky 40207

LOUISIANA
Louisiana Medical Board
830 Union Street
New Orleans, Louisiana 70112

MAINE
Maine Medical Board
State House, Room 137
Augusta, Maine 04333

MARYLAND
Maryland Medical Board
P.O. Box 2571
Baltimore, Maryland 21215

MASSACHUSETTS
Massachusetts Medical Board
10 West Street
Boston, Massachusetts 02111

MICHIGAN
Michigan Medical Board
P.O. Box 30018
Lansing, Michigan 48909

MINNESOTA
Minnesota Medical Board
2700 University Avenue, West
Saint Paul, Minnesota 55114

MISSISSIPPI
Mississippi Medical Board
2688 Insurance Center Drive
Jackson, Mississippi 39216

MISSOURI
Missouri Medical Board
P.O. Box 4
Jefferson City, Missouri 65102

MONTANA
Montana Medical Board
1424 9th Avenue
Helena, Montana 59620

NEBRASKA
Nebraska Medical Board
P.O. Box 95007
Lincoln, Nebraska 68509

NEVADA
Nevada Medical Board
P.O. Box 7238
Reno, Nevada 89510

NEW HAMPSHIRE
New Hampshire Medical Board
6 Hazen Drive
Concord, New Hampshire 03301

NEW JERSEY
New Jersey Medical Board
28 West State Street
Trenton, New Jersey 08608

NEW MEXICO
New Mexico Medical Board
P.O. Box 20001
Santa Fe, New Mexico 87504

NEW YORK
New York Medical Board
Empire State Plaza, Room 3023
Albany, New York 12230

NORTH CAROLINA
North Carolina Medical Board
1313 Navaho Drive
Raleigh, North Carolina 27609

NORTH DAKOTA
North Dakota Medical Board
418 East Broadway
Bismarck, North Dakota 58501

OHIO
Ohio Medical Board
77 South High Street
Columbus, Ohio 43266

OKLAHOMA
Oklahoma Medical Board
P.O. Box 18256
Oklahoma City, Oklahoma 73154

OREGON
Oregon Medical Board
620 Crown Avenue
Portland, Oregon 97201

PENNSYLVANIA
Pennsylvania Medical Board
P.O. Box 2649
Harrisburg, Pennsylvania 17105

PUERTO RICO
Puerto Rico Medical Board
P.O. Box 13969
Santurce, Puerto Rico 00908

RHODE ISLAND
Rhode Island Medical Board
3 Capital Hill Road
Providence, Rhode Island 02908

SOUTH CAROLINA
South Carolina Medical Board
Post Office Box 12245
Columbia, South Carolina 29211

SOUTH DAKOTA
South Dakota Medical Board
1323 South Minnesota Avenue
Sioux Falls, South Dakota 57105

TENNESSEE
Tennessee Medical Board
283 Plus Park Road
Nashville, Tennessee 37247

TEXAS
Texas Medical Board
P.O. Box 13562
Austin, Texas 78711

UTAH
Utah Medical Board
P.O. Box 45802
Salt Lake City, Utah 84145

VERMONT
Vermont Medical Board
Pavilion Building, Room 100
Montpelier, Vermont 05609

VIRGINIA
Virginia Medical Board
1601 Rolling Hills Drive
Richmond, Virginia 23229

WASHINGTON
Washington Medical Board
1300 Quince Street
Olympia, Washington 98504

WEST VIRGINIA
West Virginia Medical Board
101 Dee Drive
Charleston, West Virginia 25311

WISCONSIN
Wisconsin Medical Board
P.O. Box 8935
Madison, Wisconsin 53708

WYOMING
Wyoming Medical Board
2301 Central Avenue
Cheyenne, Wyoming 82002

CHAPTER SIX

HIDDEN ASSET SEARCHES

A PI is often requested to determine whether or not a person has any assets they are hiding from their creditors, from the courts, from their spouses, or other parties. An understanding of the state's laws needs to be acquired to determine whether or not finding hidden assets will ultimately do any good. Unless one spouse is searching for assets that the other may be hiding from them, all other searches should be done with specific detail to records under the name of the spouse or of relatives. For example, if a man has a business and he attempts to hide assets from his creditors, he may hide assets in his wife's name (depending on the state's laws concerning common-law property) or in the name of their children, his parents, a brother, sister, or other relative.

Where's The Money? I became involved in a particular case one day when a client called the office in a near hysterical state. The client represented a financial institution who had loaned $750,000 to a man on a "signature loan". The subject was supposed to use the money to build a business center. However, before giving the subject the last draw of $100,000 on the loan, the client sent an appraiser to the site to determine the condition and progress of the job. The client found that no work had even been started, much less nearly completed. According to the client, the subject was in the same area and did not appear to have run off with the money. The client therefore requested that I go to a nearby state (where the subject was allegedly building the structure) and determine where the money was hidden. Once I initiated the investigation, I found that there were two subjects by the same name (uncommon name) listed in the records. The information I gathered placed him as having conducted business transactions in North Carolina and back in Texas. A record I found in the deed records involved a lien and lawsuit involving a money dispute between another financial institution. The client requested that I return to Texas and follow up on the records I had found reference to. This resulted in additional findings concerning financial disputes, property ownership, and transactions in North Carolina. These records also confirmed what the social security prefix had shown, that the subject originated from North Carolina. The client demanded that I travel to North Carolina and continue the search. I eventually found records providing relative's names and determined that the money had been deposited in a small bank in the subject's home town. Through these searches, I also confirmed that the subject had been married six times, and was apparently married to two wives at the same time. The irony of this situation is that this could have been avoided if the client had requested a background investigation before loaning such a large amount of money.

A good place to start a hidden assets investigation is by checking the Bankruptcy Court Records, which handle a specific geographic area. For example, the Western District Bankruptcy Court of the State of Texas handles the San Antonio and surrounding areas. Some states have a telephone number which can be dialed and a message will guide you through a name search using the keypad to type in the person's name. The case number, dates involved, persons involved, attorneys, and other pertinent information will be provided. You should then go to the court and review the file to determine personal information, properties, stocks, art, vessels, safety deposit boxes, and other assets.

The court records will reflect all accounts in which money is owed. Because of the nature of this case, you will have the person's social security number, date of birth and all other pertinent information. It is then very easy to call the creditors and determine balances on the accounts and their status. The court records provide the account numbers for creditors and banks, and most can be searched over the telephone by simply punching in the account numbers. Information on insurance policies which have a "cash value" will also normally be listed along with the policy number. With just a few quick calls, you can determine if the account is still active and the amounts involved.

Next, the County Deed Records should be reviewed. They are generally located in the courthouse and are free of charge to access. A search by name will reveal any property owned by the subject or company. The records will give the property address, the person that they purchased the property from, the amount of the loan and hopefully the mortgage company (if applicable). In addition, the records also list tax liens, inheritances, and other pertinent information. These are good sources of information because inheritance records will reflect relative's names, where they lived (probably another county or state), what the subject inherited, and any conditions associated with the inheritance. This group of records is usually listed together in the deed records and also contain information such as "mechanics liens". These are filed by a mechanic or contractor against the vehicle or property. A lien is placed on the property which prohibit it from being sold or transferred to anyone else until the contractor is paid in full.

Garnishment records are often times listed in these records as well. This may lead you to other locations that need to be searched. For instance, if a man divorced his wife in California and the court ordered him to pay child support, he may have moved to another state so that the court would not "garnish" or require his employer to withhold the money from his check. However, once the court catches up to him in the location he moved, the court will file a "garnishment" document with the appropriate county. This type of person, if intent on not paying support, will probably be working jobs that allow them to get paid by cash so that they can hide their earnings.

Typically, some or all of the following records may be listed in the "deed record indexes" and may all be worth researching:

- Assumption agreements
- Abstract records
- Affidavits
- Agreements
- Assignments
- Breach of contracts
- Certificates
- Certificate of title
- Change of Name
- Condominium rider
- Corporation records
- Declaration of trust
- Deed records
- Discharge records
- Disclaimers
- Easement records
- Estate records
- Fictitious names
- Foreclosure records
- Guardianship records
- Tax warrants
- Support agreements
- Trust agreement
- Trustee resignation
- Incompetency proceedings
- Incorporation records
- Involuntary bankruptcy
- Judgements
- Leases
- Mortgage modifications
- Name restorations
- Nontaxable certificate
- Notice of tax liens
- Power of attorney
- Release of tax liens
- Resolutions
- Satisfaction of decree
- Satisfaction of mortgage
- Mechanic's liens
- Writ of garnishment

The County Financing Statements are located in the county clerks office of the courthouse and are free to search. The records provide a list of assets for a business used as collateral and other business transactions. A search by name can be done, resulting in the creditor, date of filing, and other useful information being revealed. The creditor can be called using a suitable pre-text form of questioning to determine if the property used as collateral is now free and clear.

The County Appraisal District is located in or near the courthouse and for no charge will provide the name of the owner, the legal description of the property, the value of the property, and usually the mortgage company. A suitable pre-text form of questioning can be used to contact the mortgage company to determine whether or not the loan has been paid off.

A review of the County's Tax Assessor's Records, which is located in the courthouse and is free of charge, can be searched by name. The records indicate any property owned, taxes due, and the mortgage company. The records should also be searched even if the subject owns a business, but not the property, because taxes have to be paid on assets such as equipment.

The County's Assumed Name Records should be searched and is in the county clerk's office generally located in the courthouse and is free of charge to the public. The records list any businesses owned by a subject, the owners, the business and owner's addresses and other useful information. A search of all records using the company name and their business partners should then be made.

The State Department of Parks and Wildlife/Game Wardens Office should be searched to determine any boats listed to the subject. The headquarters are located in the capitol city of the state but there are usually branch offices in larger cities, and there is no charge to the public. The search will provide the vessels registration number, type and size of boat, engine information, owner information, and sometimes a lienholder. The Department of Parks and Wildlife regulates hunting and fishing

Boat Search

Subject: ______________________________

____

____

Jurisdiction: ______________________________

A search has been conducted on the above referenced subject and the following information was obtained.

Boats

John J. Doe
888 SW 22nd Street
Miami, FL 33222

1988 Bertram
37′
Documented with the U.S. Coast Gard
Document #: B00222
Hul #: DEVW0221D8

licenses and those subjects who are attempting to hide, sometimes get these licenses to avoid confrontation with authorities while involved in these sports.

A search of the State's Department of Aviation/FAA, which is usually headquartered in the capitol city of the state should be made. There is no charge to the public and a name search will reveal any airplanes owned by the subject or their company. In addition, the aircraft information, the location where it is commonly sheltered, and other information can be obtained. In some states, the Department of Parks and Wildlife or the State Department of Transportation may also oversee these records.

The State's Railroad Commission, also located in the capitol city of the state, provides free-of-charge searches for the public. The information can tell you if the subject or company is licensed to transport materials through their system. The amount of information obtained is often minimal, but can provide some beneficial material.

The Secretary of State's Office is located in the capitol city and provides searches free of charge. They should be contacted to determine whether there are any companies listed to the subject. Often, the Secretary of State can only search under a company name. However, the records will provide the registered agent, owners, officers, all addresses, the date of incorporation, and other useful information.

The State Comptroller's Office will search by a subject's name or a company name and is free of charge to the public. Any business operating in the state is required to pay taxes to the state. The material can provide information related to taxes paid on inheritances, mineral rights, oil and gas wells, interstate transportation franchise taxes, hotel taxes, and amusement taxes.

A search of the County's District Civil Records and the County Civil Records should be conducted. The district clerk's office oversees the district civil records which involves property or damages above $1,000. The county clerk's office oversees the county civil records which involves property or damages under $1,000. Both are generally housed at the courthouse and searches are free of charge to the public. A name search will reveal any lawsuits involving the subject which typically includes divorces, child support, automobile damages, workers compensation cases, and various other types of litigation. Once a match is found, the actual file should be requested from the clerk. File material typically provides personal information, assets involved in divorce cases, amount of child support being paid, amount of settlements in cases, and other pertinent information.

The State Department of Transportation located in the capitol city of the state, often has a telephone number dedicated to conducting searches for the public. A name search can be conducted to determine any vehicles registered to the subject, their license plate numbers, and other useful information.

The County Birth Records are maintained by the county clerk's office in the courthouse. Recently, several states and/or counties have restricted access to these records due to foster children and adoptions. However, this is still a good source to consider. You can confirm whether or not the person was born locally, confirm their date of birth or legal name, and determine the names of their parents. If the date of birth or legal name is different or slightly altered, this may have a direct bearing on the success of the record checks.

A search of the "Brand" Indexes should be considered if the area is known for maintaining livestock. The indexes are usually kept in the county clerk's office at the courthouse and are generally listed in alphabetical books and are not on computer. It is common for ranchers to register a brand that they use on their cattle or livestock and the information may lead to a ranching business that was previously undiscovered.

Bankruptcy Courts

ALABAMA
United States Bankruptcy Court
500 S. 22nd St.
Birmingham, Alabama 35233
United States Bankruptcy Court
P.O. Box 1248
Montgomery, Alabama 36192
United States Bankruptcy Court
P.O. Box 2865
Mobile, Alabama 36652

ALASKA
United States Bankruptcy Court
222 W. 7th Ave.
Anchorage, Alaska 99513

ARIZONA
United States Bankruptcy Court
230 North 1st Ave.
Phoenix, Arizona 85025
United States Bankruptcy court
110 South Church
Tucson, Arizona 85702

ARKANSAS
United States Bankruptcy Court
P.O. Box 2381
Little Rock, Arkansas 72203

CALIFORNIA
United States Bankruptcy Court
312 N. Spring St.
Los Angeles, California 90012
United States Bankruptcy Court
940 Front St.
San Diego, California 92189
United States Bankruptcy Court
1130 O Street
Fresno, California, 93721
United States Bankruptcy Court
450 Golden Gate Ave.
San Francisco, California 94102
United States Bankruptcy Court
P. O. Box 5276
Modesto, California 95352

COLORADO
United States Bankruptcy Court
1845 Sherman St.
Denver, Colorado 80203

CONNECTICUT
United States Bankruptcy Court
450 Main St.
Hartford, Connecticut 06103

DELAWARE
United States Bankruptcy Court
844 N. King St.
Wilmington, Delaware 19801

DISTRICT OF COLUMBIA
United States Bankruptcy Court
300 Constitution Ave., Northwest
Washington, D.C. 20001

FLORIDA
United States Bankruptcy Court
51 Southwest 1st Ave.
Miami, Florida 33101
United States Bankruptcy Court
299 E. Broward Blvd.
Fort Lauderdale, Florida 33301
United States Bankruptcy Court
227 N. Bronough St.
Tallahassee, Florida 32301
United States Bankruptcy Court
4921 Memorial Highway
Tampa, Florida 33634
United States Bankruptcy Court
P. O. Box 559
Jacksonville, Florida 32201

GEORGIA
United States Bankruptcy Court
P. O. Box 1957
Macon, Georgia 31202
United States Bankruptcy Court
75 Spring St.
Atlanta, Georgia 30303
United States
Bankruptcy Court
P. O. Box 8347
Savannah, Georgia 31412

HAWAII
United States Bankruptcy Court
P. O. Box 50121
Honolulu, Hawaii 96850

IDAHO
United States Bankruptcy Court
P. O. Box 2600
Boise, Idaho 83701

ILLINOIS
United States Bankruptcy Court
219 S. Dearborn St.
Chicago, Illinois 60604
United States Bankruptcy Court
P. O. Box 309
East Saint Louis, Illinois 62201
United States Bankruptcy Court
P. O. Box 2438
Springfield, Illinois 62705

INDIANA
United States Bankruptcy Court
46 East Ohio St.
Indianapolis, Indiana 46204
United States Bankruptcy Court
610 Connecticut St.
Gary, Indiana 46402
United States Bankruptcy Court
204 S. Main St.
South Bend, Indiana 46601

IOWA
United States Bankruptcy Court
1 Walnut St.
Des Moines, Iowa 50309

KANSAS
United States Bankruptcy Court
401 N. Market St.
Wichita, Kansas 67202

KENTUCKY
United States Bankruptcy Court
601 W. Broadway
Louisville, Kentucky 40202
United States Bankruptcy Court
P. O. Box 1050
Lexington, Kentucky 40588

LOUISIANA
United States Bankruptcy Court
500 Camp St.
New Orleans, Louisiana 70130
United States Bankruptcy Court
412 N. 4th St.
Baton Rouge, Louisiana 70802
United States Bankruptcy Court
500 Fannin St.
Shreveport, Louisiana 71109

MAINE
United States Bankruptcy Court
156 Federal Way
Portland, Maine 04112

MARYLAND
United States Bankruptcy Court
101 W. Lombard St.
Baltimore, Maryland 21201

MASSACHUSETTS
United States Bankruptcy Court
10 Causeway
Boston, Massachusetts 02222

MICHIGAN
United States Bankruptcy Court
231 W. LaFayette St.
Detroit, Michigan 48226
United States Bankruptcy Court
P. O. Box 3310
Grand Rapids, Michigan 49501

MINNESOTA
United States Bankruptcy Court
316 N. Robert St.
Saint Paul, Minnesota 55101
United States Bankruptcy Court
330 2nd Ave.
Minneapolis, Minnesota 55401

MISSISSIPPI
United States Bankruptcy Court
245 E. Capitol St.
Jackson, Mississippi 39201
United States Bankruptcy Court
P. O. Box 369
Biloxi, Mississippi 39533
United States Bankruptcy Court
P. O. Box 867
Averdeen, Mississippi 39730

MISSOURI
United States Bankruptcy Court
1114 Market St.
Saint Louis, Missouri 63101
United States Bankruptcy Court
811 Grand Ave.
Kansas City, Missouri 64106

MONTANA
United States Bankruptcy Court
273 Federal Building
Butte, Montana 59701

NEBRASKA
United States Bankruptcy Court
P. O. Box 428
Omaha, Nebraska 68101

NEVADA
United States Bankruptcy Court
300 Las Vegas Boulevard
Las Vegas, Nevada 89101

NEW HAMPSHIRE
United States Bankruptcy Court
275 Chestnut St.
Manchester, New Hampshire 03101

NEW JERSEY
United States Bankruptcy Court
15 North 7 St.
Camden, New Jersey 08102
United States Bankruptcy Court
P. O. Box 515
Trenton, New Jersey 08603

NEW MEXICO
United States Bankruptcy Court
P. O. Box 546
Albuquerque, New Mexico 87103

NEW YORK
United States Bankruptcy Court
1 Bowling Green
New York, New York 10004
United States Bankruptcy Court
75 Clinton St.
Brooklyn, New York 11201
United States Bankruptcy Court
P. O. Box 398
Albany, New York 12201
United States Bankruptcy Court
68 Court St.
Buffalo, New York 14202
United States Bankruptcy Court
100 State St.
Rochester, New York 14614

NORTH CAROLINA
United States Bankruptcy Court
P. O. Box 26100
Greensboro, North Carolina 27420
United States Bankruptcy Court
P. O. Box 2807
Wilson, North Carolina 27894
United States Bankruptcy Court
100 Otis St.
Asheville, North Carolina 28801

NORTH DAKOTA
United States Bankruptcy Court
P. O. Box 1110
Fargo, North Dakota 58107

OHIO
United States Bankruptcy Court
1716 Spielbusch Ave.
Toledo, Ohio 43624
United States Bankruptcy Court
201 Superior Ave.
Cleveland, Ohio 44114
United States Bankruptcy Court
2 South Main St.
Akron, Ohio 44308
United States Bankruptcy Court
9 West Front St.
Youngstown, Ohio 44501
United States Bankruptcy Court
201 Cleveland Ave.
Canton, Ohio 44702
United States Bankruptcy Court
85 Marconi Blvd.
Columbus, Ohio 43215

OKLAHOMA
United States Bankruptcy Court
201 Dean McGee Ave.
Oklahoma City, Oklahoma 73102
United States Bankruptcy Court
111 W. Fifth St.
Tulsa, Oklahoma 74103
United States Bankruptcy Court
P. O. Box 1347
Okmulgee, Oklahoma 74447

OREGON
United States Bankruptcy Court
P. O. Box 1335
Eugene, Oregon 97440

United States Bankruptcy Court
1001 S.W. Fifth Ave.
Portland, Oregon, 97204

PENNSYLVANIA
United States Bankruptcy Court
1602 Liberty Ave.
Pittsburgh, Pennsylvania 15222
United States Bankruptcy Court
197 S. Main St.
Wilkes Barre, Pennsylvania 18701
United States Bankruptcy Court
601 Market St.
Philadelphia, Pennsylvania 19106

RHODE ISLAND
United States Bankruptcy Court
380 Westminster Mall
Providence, Rhode Island 02903

SOUTH CAROLINA
United States Bankruptcy Court
P. O. Box 1448
Columbia, South Carolina 29202

SOUTH DAKOTA
United States Bankruptcy Court
P. O. Box 5060
Sioux Falls, South Dakota 57117

TENNESSEE
United States Bankruptcy Court
701 Broadway
Nashville, Tennessee 37203
United States Bankruptcy Court
P. O. Box 2348
Knoxville, Tennessee 37901
United States Bankruptcy Court
969 Madison Ave.
Memphis, Tennessee 38104

TEXAS
United States Bankruptcy Court
1100 Commerce St.
Dallas, Texas 75242
United States Bankruptcy Court
211 W. Ferguson St.
Tyler, Texas 75702
United States Bankruptcy Court
501 W. 10th St.
Fort Worth, Texas 76102
United States Bankruptcy Court
1205 Texas Ave.
Lubbock, Texas 79401
United States Bankruptcy Court
515 Rusk Ave.
Houston, Texas 77002
United States Bankruptcy Court
P. O. Box 1439
San Antonio, Texas 78295

UTAH
United States Bankruptcy Court
350 S. Main St.
Salt Lake City, Utah 84101

VERMONT
United States Bankruptcy Court
P. O. Box 6648
Rutland, Vermont 05702

VIRGINIA
United States Bankruptcy Court
206 N. Washington St.
Alexandria, Virginia 22314
United States Bankruptcy Court
P. O. Box 676
Richmond, Virginia 23206
United States Bankruptcy Court
600 Granby St.
Norfolk, Virginia 23510
United States Bankruptcy Court
P. O. Box 497
Newport News, Virginia 23607
United States Bankruptcy Court
P. O. Box 2390
Roanoke, Virginia 24010

WASHINGTON
United States Bankruptcy Court
1200 Sixth Ave.
Seattle, Washington 98101
United States Bankruptcy Court
P. O. Box 2164
Spokane, Washington 99201

WEST VIRGINIA
United States Bankruptcy Court
P. O. Box 3924
Charleston, West Virginia 25301
United States Bankruptcy Court
P. O. Box 70
Wheeling, West Virginia 26003

WISCONSIN
United States Bankruptcy Court
517 W. Wisconsin Ave.
Milwaukee, Wisconsin 53202
United States Bankruptcy Court
P. O. Box 548
Madison, Wisconsin 53701

WYOMING
United States Bankruptcy Court
P. O. Box 1107
Cheyenne, Wyoming 82003

Depending on the nature of the subject's business, you may desire to check with the Commission of Patents and Trademarks. If the subject has an idea, invention, or trademark, they may have filed this information with the office to protect against competition. A person can be listed on a patent if they were the engineer or major contributor to the project. Therefore, if you suspect that the subject has expertise in a particular area (Ex: engineering, science, etc.), you may want to research this. This in turn, can lead to the name, businesses and associates who may have assets related to the subject. You can research this information by writing the Patent and Trademark Office, Washington, D. C. 20231 or by calling (703) 308-4357.

The office of the International Trademark Association, 1133 Avenue of the America's, New York, N.Y. 10036 or (212) 768-9886, should be searched if you suspect a trademark protection has been applied for to obtain international protection.

Depending on the nature of your inquiry, you may want to contact the Bureau of the Public Debt, Savings Bonds Operations Office, at 200 Third Street, Parkersburg, W. V. 26106-1328. This search will advise you whether or not there are any unclaimed U. S. Savings Bonds. The government has approximately $1.7 billion in unredeemed, matured savings bonds.

Additionally, the State's Treasury Department, (State Comptroller or Department of Revenue in some states) regulates unclaimed monies from old bank accounts, tax refunds, uncollected insurance polices, etc. Most people are not aware that the contents of a safe deposit box can be seized and held if there is no activity for 3-5 years.

SECRETARY OF STATE
AUSTIN, TEXAS

DETERMINATION OF FORFEITURE PURSUANT TO SECTION 171.309, TEXAS TAX CODE ANNOTATED

CAME TO BE CONSIDERED ON THE DATE SHOWN HEREON, FORFEITURE OF THE CHARTER OR CERTIFICATE OF AUTHORITY OF THE FOLLOWING CORPORATION; THE SECRETARY OF STATE FINDS AND DETERMINES THE FOLLOWING:

CORPORATION NAME

UTURO FARMS, INC.

CHARTER NO.-TYPE	RTDB FORFEITED	CERTIFICATE/CHARTER FORFEITED
05638-00	08/21/1987	01/18/1988

THAT THE COMPTROLLER OF PUBLIC ACCOUNTS HAS NOTIFIED THIS OFFICE THAT SAID CORPORATION HAS FAILED TO FILE A CURRENT YEAR FRANCHISE TAX REPORT TO ESTABLISH THE EXISTENCE OF ASSETS FROM WHICH A JUDGEMENT FOR THE FRANCHISE TAXES, PENALTIES AND COURT COSTS MAY BE SATISFIED.
THAT THE COMPTROLLER OF PUBLIC ACCOUNTS HAS FURTHER STATED THAT THE SAID CORPORATION HAS FAILED OR REFUSED TO REVIVE ITS RIGHT TO DO BUSINESS.

IT IS THEREFORE ORDERED THAT THE CHARTER OR CERTIFICATE OF AUTHORITY OF THE ABOVE NAMED CORPORATION BE AND THE SAME IS HEREBY FORFEITED WITHOUT JUDICIAL ASCERTAINMENT AND MADE NULL AND VOID, AND THAT THE PROPER ENTRY BE MADE UPON THE PERMANENT FILES AND RECORDS OF SUCH CORPORATION TO SHOW SUCH FORFEITURE AS OF THE DATE HEREOF.

The Department of Veteran's Affairs is also a source to check to determine if there are any unclaimed benefits owed to veterans and their families. You can call 1-800-829-1040 to initiate the search.

The Office of Personnel Management oversees benefits due to former Federal employees and their spouses and currently have several millions in unclaimed benefits. To search, write to the office at the "Retirement Operations Center", Boyers, PA 16017

The Military Service. Each branch of the military has a Military Locator Service which you can write to if the subject or relative is believed to be in or formerly in the military. You can learn the rank, duty assignments (past and present) with office telephone numbers, decorations and honors and other useful information. Each branch (Air Force, Army, etc.) have these offices within their branches and are usually in Washington, D. C.

By the time all of these searches are conducted, you should have a pretty good grasp of the person's financial status. However, if this information is not sufficient, other alternatives may need to be considered and will be discussed later in this book.

Vehicles Registration and Title Offices

ALABAMA
Dept. of Motor Vehicles
State of Alabama
P.O. Box 104
Montgomery, Alabama 36101

ALASKA
Dept. of Motor Vehicles
State of Alaska
5700 Todor Rd
Anchorage, Alaska 99507

ARIZONA
Dept. of Motor Vehicles
State of Arizona
1801 W. Jefferson St.
Phoenix, Arizona 85001

ARKANSAS
Dept. of Motor Vehicles
State of Arkansas
P.O. 1272
Little Rock, Arkansas 72203

CALIFORNIA
Dept. of Motor Vehicles
State of California
P.O. Box 932328
Sacramento, California 94232

COLORADO
Dept. of Motor Vehicles
State of Colorado
140 W. 6th St.
Denver, Colorado 80204

CONNECTICUT
Dept. of Motor Vehicles
State of Connecticut
60 State St.
Wethersfield, Connecticut 06109

DELAWARE
Dept. of Motor Vehicles
State of Delaware
State Office Building
Dover, Delaware 19903

DISTRICT OF COLUMBIA
Dept. of Motor Vehicles
District of Columbia
301 C Street
Washington, D.C. 20001

FLORIDA
Dept. of Motor Vehicles
State of Florida
2900 Apalachee Parkway
Tallahassee, Florida 32399

GEORGIA
Dept. of Motor Vehicles
State of Georgia
104 Trinty Washington Building
Atlanta, Georgia 30334

HAWAII
Dept. of Motor Vehicles
State of Hawaii
896 Punchbowl St.
Honolulu, Hawaii 96813

IDAHO
Dept. of Motor Vehicles
State of Idaho
P.O. Box 34
Boise, Idaho 83731

ILLINOIS
Dept. of Motor Vehicles
State of Illinois
Centennial Government Building
Springfield, Illinois 62756

INDIANA
Dept. of Motor Vehicles
State of Indiana
State Office Building, Room 416
Indianapolis, Indiana 46204

IOWA
Dept. of Motor Vehicles
State of Iowa
Park Fair Mall, Box 9204
Des Moines, Iowa 50306

KANSAS
Dept. of Motor Vehicles
State of Kansas
P.O. Box 12021
Topeka, Kansas 66616

KENTUCKY
Dept. of Motor Vehicles
State of Kentucky
State Building, Room 204
Frankfort, Kentucky 40622

LOUISIANA
Dept. of Motor Vehicles
State of Louisiana
P. O. Box 64886
Baton Rouge, Louisiana 70896

MAINE
Dept. of Motor Vehicles
State of Maine
State Building
Augusta, Maine 04333

MARYLAND
Dept. of Motor Vehicles
State of Maryland
6601 Ritchie Highway, N.E.
Glen Burnie, Maryland 21062

MASSACHUSETTS
Dept. of Motor Vehicles
State of Massachusetts
100 Nashua St., Room 100
Boston, Massachusetts 02114

MICHIGAN
Dept. of Motor Vehicles
State of Michigan
Mutual Government Building
Lansing, Michigan 48918

MINNESOTA
Dept. of Motor Vehicles
State of Minnesota
Transportation Building, Room 159
Saint Paul, Minnesota 55155

MISSISSIPPI
Dept. of Motor Vehicles
State of Mississippi
P.O. Box 1140
Jackson, Mississippi 39205

MISSOURI
Dept. of Motor Vehicles
State of Missouri
P.O. Box 100
Jefferson City, Missouri 65105

MONTANA
Dept. of Motor Vehicles
State of Montana
925 Main St.
Deer Lodge, Montana 59722

NEBRASKA
Dept. of Motor Vehicles
State of Nebraska
P.O. Box 94789
Lincoln, Nebraska 68509

NEVADA
Dept. of Motor Vehicles
State of Nevada
State Building
Carson City, Nevada 89111

NEW HAMPSHIRE
Dept. of Motor Vehicles
State of New Hampshire
James H. Hayes Building
Concord, New Hampshire 03305

NEW JERSEY
Dept. of Motor Vehicles
State of New Jersey
135 E. State St.
Trenton, New Jersey 08666

NEW MEXICO
Dept. of Motor Vehicles
State of New Mexico
P.O. Box 1028
Santa Fe, New Mexico 87504

NEW YORK
Dept. of Motor Vehicles
State of New York
State Office Building North
Albany, New York 12228

NORTH CAROLINA
Dept. of Motor Vehicles
State of North Carolina
1100 New Bern Ave., Room 124
Raleigh, North Carolina 27697

NORTH DAKOTA
Dept. of Motor Vehicles
State of North Dakota
806 East Boulevard
Bismarck, North Dakota 58505

OHIO
Dept. of Motor Vehicles
State of Ohio
P.O. Box 16520
Columbus, Ohio 43266

OKLAHOMA
Dept. of Motor Vehicles
State of Oklahoma
409 Northeast 28 St.
Oklahoma City, Oklahoma 73105

OREGON
Dept. of Motor Vehicles
State of Oregon
1905 Lana Ave., N.E.
Salem, Oregon 97314

PENNSYLVANIA
Dept. of Motor Vehicles
State of Pennsylvania
P.O. Box 8691
Harrisburg, Pennsylvania 17105

PUERTO RICO
Dept. of Motor Vehicles
Commonwealth of Puerto Rico
P.O. Box 41269
Santurce, Puerto Rico 00940

RHODE ISLAND
Dept. of Motor Vehicles
State of Rhode Island
State Office Building
Providence, Rhode Island 02903

SOUTH CAROLINA
Dept. of Motor Vehicles
State of South Carolina
P.O. Box 1498
Columbia, South Carolina 29216

SOUTH DAKOTA
Dept. of Motor Vehicles
State of South Dakota
118 W. Capitol Ave.
Columbia, South Dakota 57501

TENNESSEE
Dept. of Motor Vehicles
State of Tennessee
500 Deaderick St.
Nashville, Tennessee 37242

TEXAS
Dept. of Motor Vehicles
State of Texas
5805 N. Lamar Boulevard
Austin, Texas 78773

UTAH
Dept. of Motor Vehicles
State of Utah
1095 Motor Ave.
Salt Lake City, Utah 84116

VERMONT
Dept. of Motor Vehicles
State of Vermont
120 State St.
Montpelier, Vermont 05603

VIRGINIA
Dept. of Motor Vehicles
State of Virginia
P.O. Box 27412
Richmond, Virginia 23269

WASHINGTON
Dept. of Motor Vehicles
State of Washington
P. O. Box 9909
Olympia, Washington 98504

WEST VIRGINIA
Dept. of Motor Vehicles
State of West Virginia
State Office Building
Charleston, West Virginia 25305

WISCONSIN
Dept. of Motor Vehicles
State of Wisconsin
4802 Sheboygan Ave.
Madison, Wisconsin 53707

WYOMING
Dept. of Motor Vehicles
State of Wyoming
122 W. 25th St.
Cheyenne, Wyoming 82002

CHAPTER SEVEN

BACKGROUND INVESTIGATIONS

A general background investigation is often done to determine the general character of a person or to verify information provided by a subject. A lot of the previously discussed records should be utilized to achieve the goals.

What a Friend: I received a call from a client who was concerned that a supervisor at their bank, who was soon to be promoted to Vice-President, may be embezzling money. Another supervisor had filled in for the subject one day and found some discrepancies which led them to additional discrepancies over the past three years. I immediately began to conduct general record searches as described in this book and determined that the subject was having money difficulties. I continued my search which resulted in my finding a hair salon which the subject purchased in a friend's name and backed financially. As I continued, the records revealed the subject spent a lot of time in Las Vegas. After approaching the neighbors to confirm the information, I was advised the subject regularly took her friends and family to Las Vegas for an all expense paid weekend. Unfortunately for the client, it appeared that the subject had squandered all of the money away.

It is unfortunate that in today's society, we cannot trust even the basic authority figures. A growing concern is the credentials of the daycare workers, teachers, bus drivers, little league coaches, doctors, lawyers, and others who are in a position of authority. There is an alarming increase in the number of school and church officials who are being revealed as child molesters and pornography promoters. Although teachers have to undergo a background check, there are several problems with this. First, some school districts only perform background checks on management candidates, while others perform checks on only "permanent teacher positions" which do not include substitutes, bus drivers, janitors, or cafeteria workers. Secondly, the criminal history check normally consists of the Department of Public Safety checking the N.C.I.C. computer system for criminal charges. As discussed previously, the N.C.I.C. system is not fool proof. There is at least one case known to the author in which a teacher had undergone this type of check. However, when the teacher was accused of molesting a child, it was determined that the teacher was currently awaiting trial on a similar charge. A check of the courthouse records would have divulged this information, which was not on the N.C.I.C. system.

Obviously, a parent can't check every person that your child may come into contact with. However, when there are individuals such as teachers, church officials, scout leaders, and others who hold a position of trust and who spend a significant amount of time with your child, it may warrant spending a little time to protect your child. Our society is filled with stories such as these. The church has come under scrutiny because of the number of officials who are being accused of molesting children in their parishes. Other churches are being placed in awkward situations due to their pastors having adulterous sexual affairs. The list goes on and on and no profession appears to be unaffected. There are stories of physicians molesting patients while examining them, or fleeing to a different state to practice because of disciplinary actions being presented against them in their original state of licensing. There are therapists who have been accused of taking advantage of their patient's emotional trauma. We read about police officers who use their power to exert sexual favors or who break into the businesses they are suppose to be protecting. There is the "tail-hook" scandal that took place in the military and involved sexual harassment. This is not an attack on the professions or any particular person. It is just a fact. These things are occurring around us and we can no longer believe that we or someone we know will not be affected. Just like we are being urged to become more involved in our local community, in politics, and other issues, we should also be urged to no longer take things at face value. The records and resources are available and is no longer information that is "secret" or non-retrievable.

To properly investigate someone's background, first the local County Appraisal District records should be searched. This information will tell you whether the subject owns any property, the value of the property, and any mortgage company. This will enable you to determine how stable the person is in the community, as property owners are generally interested in staying where they have purchased property. A name search or a search by address can be conducted and the office is usually located in or near the courthouse. The search can typically be conducted free of charge and several computer terminals are usually available to the public.

The County's Deed Records is another good place to search and the office is usually located in the courthouse. Several computer terminals are usually present for use by the public at no charge. A name search will reveal any property ownership, prior ownership, delinquent taxes, inheritances, oil and mineral wells, liens, and other information. This information will help form the overall picture in regards to the subjects net worth, assets, stability, and general character.

A review of the County's Tax Records can be done by conducting a name search. The office usually is located in the courthouse and several computers are normally present to conduct the searches, free of charge. The tax records provide the amount of taxes paid on any property or business equipment/assets. The information will indicate whether the taxes have been paid or are in arrears. If the taxes are delinquent, it is usually a good indicator that the subject is having financial difficulty.

The County's Marriage Records are a good source to review, depending on the nature of your search. The information may help provide you with the information needed to conduct additional searches such as their full legal name, correct date of birth, social security number, driver's license number as well as other useful facts. The records are located in the county clerk's office and are generally free of charge for the public's view. The records are searched using the person's name. If the subject is a female, their maiden name or former married name may be essential to the success of the search.

To better determine the subject's general economic condition, a check of the Bankruptcy Court Records should be conducted. The courts are usually located in the Federal building in large cities and each court covers a particular geographic area. Many of the courts have a telephone number dedicated to the public with instructions on how to use the telephone key pad to make your search. If a case is found, you will be given the case number, parties involved, dates filed, and the attorney's names. You should then go to the office and request to see the actual file. Enclosed in the records will be a tremendous amount of personal information on the subject, debts as well as a wealth of additional information. This material will provide a more complete picture of the subject's ability to manage money, their personal worth, and their general character.

Next, the Assumed Name Records should be reviewed. The records are typically part of the county clerks office and are usually located in the courthouse. Several computer terminals normally are present and the public can conduct the searches free of charge. A name search will provide you with any businesses listed to the subject, as well as the other owners and addresses. In addition, it is not unusual for a person to change their name to reflect their religion or for other reasons.

The County Criminal Records will provide a good insight into the person's criminal background. Remember that there is the district criminal records and the county criminal records. The district records involve the more serious charges, while the county records are for the lesser violations. The district criminal records are housed in the district court clerk's office, while the county criminal records are in the county clerk's office. Both are in the courthouse, can be searched by the public through computer terminals at the office, and there is typically no charge for this. The records include the arrest information, the charge itself, references to police department records, and often times provides other useful information such as relatives and employers.

The County Civil Records are useful in determining who the subject has sued, as well as who has filed a lawsuit against the subject. These cases involve delinquent debts, unpaid taxes, divorces, child support, personal injury cases, and other general cases. Again, remember, the records are provided in two places. The county's district civil records are the more serious cases and usually involve damages over $1,000. These records are located in the district court clerk's office, usually in the courthouse. The county clerk's office maintains the county civil records, which is also in the courthouse. The records can be searched by name, or case number if you know one. The material will indicate the case number, the parties involved, the type of case, and the date it was filed. You can then take the case number to one of the clerk's who will pull the file and allow you

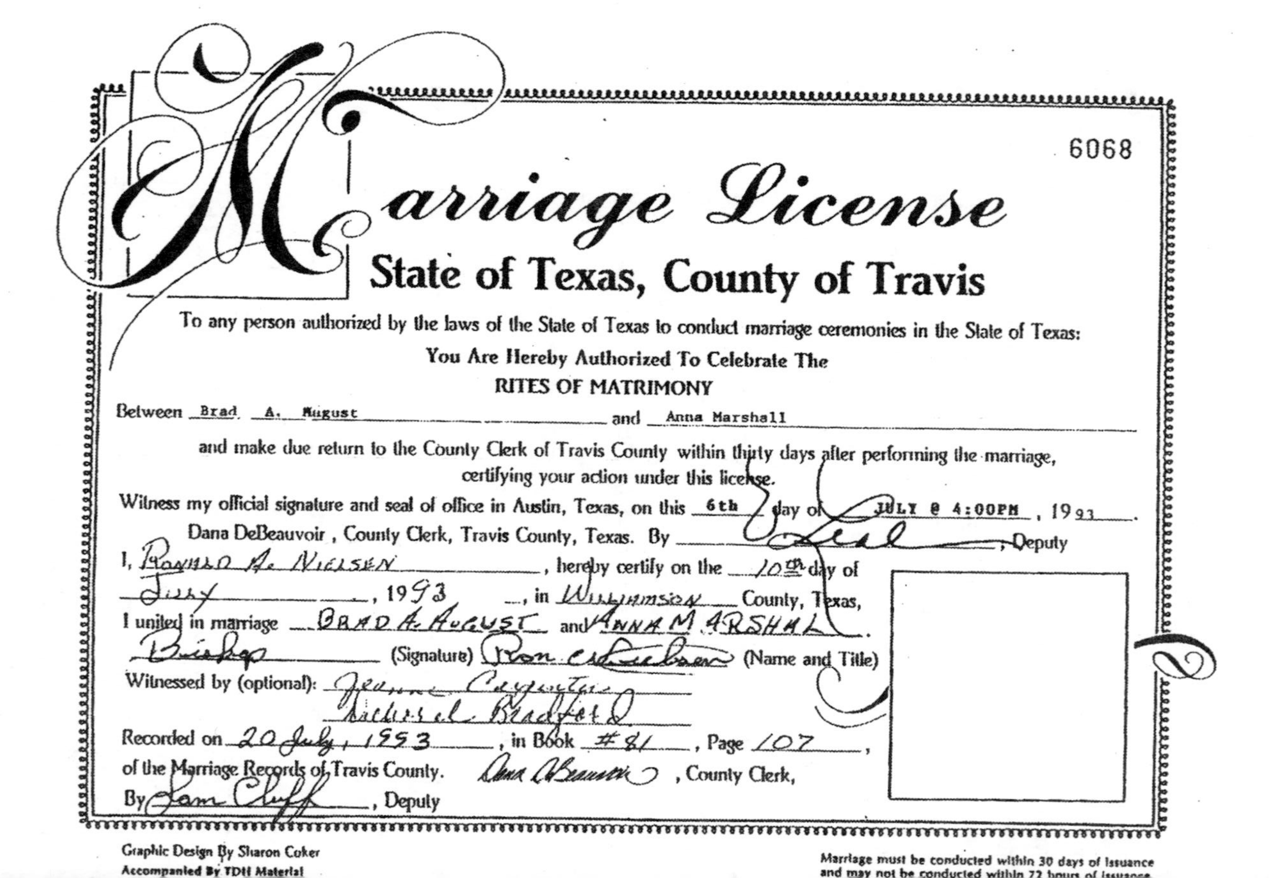

6068

Marriage License

State of Texas, County of Travis

To any person authorized by the laws of the State of Texas to conduct marriage ceremonies in the State of Texas:

You Are Hereby Authorized To Celebrate The

RITES OF MATRIMONY

Between Brad A. August and Anna Marshall

and make due return to the County Clerk of Travis County within thirty days after performing the marriage, certifying your action under this license.

Witness my official signature and seal of office in Austin, Texas, on this 6th day of JULY @ 4:00PM, 1993.

Dana DeBeauvoir, County Clerk, Travis County, Texas. By [signature], Deputy

I, Ronald A. Nielsen, hereby certify on the 10th day of July, 1993, in Williamson County, Texas, I united in marriage Brad A. August and Anna Marshal.

Bishop (Signature) Ron Nielsen (Name and Title)

Witnessed by (optional): Jeanne Carpenter

Richard L. Bradford

Recorded on 20 July, 1993, in Book #81, Page 107, of the Marriage Records of Travis County. Dana DeBeauvoir, County Clerk,

By Sam Cliff, Deputy

Graphic Design By Sharon Coker
Accompanied By TDH Material

Marriage must be conducted within 30 days of issuance and may not be conducted within 72 hours of issuance to review it. In the file, you may find personal information, debts, employers, relatives, amount of child support, vehicle information, and related data. This information will help provide insight into the person's responsibilities towards his family, debts, and the community in general.

The Better Business Bureau should be contacted if you are checking on a person who owns a company, or if you are checking on the company itself. These offices are located in most major cities and will indicate if there have been any complaints against the company. These searches can be done over the telephone and are free of charge.

A check with a related State Board should be considered if the subject is a member of a profession that licenses individuals. These include doctors (who also have state boards for specialties), insurance agents, dentists, chiropractors, therapists, pharmacists, psychologists, police officers, security guards, attorneys, real estate agents (also have local boards), taxi drivers, pilots, teachers, and various other professions. The State Boards are usually located in the capitol city of the state and will conduct a search by the person's name over the telephone. They can confirm that the person holds a license, when it was issued, colleges they attended, business addresses, and sometimes the person's date of birth and/or social security number. The board can also advise whether or not the subject had any complaints filed against them as well as their status.

The County Birth Records are maintained by the county clerk's office in the courthouse. Recently, several states and/or counties have restricted access to these records due to foster children and adoptions, but this is still a source to consider. You can confirm whether or not the person was born locally, confirm their date of birth, confirm their legal name, and determine the name of their parents. If the date of birth or legal name is different or slightly altered, this may have a direct bearing on the success of the record checks.

ASSUMED NAME CERTIFICATE

(FOR AN UNINCORPORATED BUSINESS)

PURSUANT TO THE PROVISION OF CHAPTER 36, TITLE 4, BUSINESS AND COMMERCE CODE OF THE STATE OF TEXAS, THE UNDERSIGNED CERTIFIES THE FOLLOWING:

1. THE ASSUMED NAME AND ITS BUSINESS ADDRESS UNDER WHICH THE BUSINESS IS NOW OR IS TO BE CONDUCTED IS:

ASSUMED NAME	BUSINESS ADDRESS
CRY WORKS	RT. 7 Box 68 Canyon Lake, Texas 78133

2. CHECK ONE: [ ] INDIVIDUAL [X] GENERAL PARTNERSHIP [ ] LIMITED PARTNERSHIP [ ] ESTATE [ ] REAL ESTATE INVESTMENT TRUST

NAME (S)	RESIDENCE ADDRESS (ES)
Michael Scott	13702 Castle San Antonio, Texas 78231
Raymond Keith	Rt. 8 Box 68 Canyon Lake, Texas 78133

3. THE PERIOD, NOT TO EXCEED TEN YEARS, DURING WHICH THE ASSUMED NAME WILL BE USED IS FROM THE DATE FILED WITH THE COUNTY CLERK.

IN TESTIMONY WHEREOF, We HAVE HEREUNTO SET OUR HAND (S) THIS THE ______ DAY OF MAR. 6 1989, 19______

SIGNATURE (S)

Michael Scott TDL 061803

Raymond Keith TDL 124354

THE STATE OF TEXAS I

COUNTY OF BEXAR I

BEFORE ME, THE UNDERSIGNED AUTHORITY, ON THIS DAY PERSONALLY APPEARED Michael Scott and Raymond Keith

KNOWN TO ME TO BE THE PERSON(S) WHOSE NAME(S) SUBSCRIBED TO THE FOREGOING INSTRUMENT AND ACKNOWLEDGED TO ME THAT ____HE(Y) EXECUTED THE SAME FOR THE PURPOSE AND CONSIDERATION THEREIN EXPRESSED.

GIVEN UNDER MY HAND AND SEAL OF OFFICE, THIS MAR. 6 1989 DAY OF ______ 19______.

NOTARY PUBLIC, STATE OF TEXAS
Martha Guyewski
MY COMMISSION EXPIRES Notary Public, State of Texas
My Commission Expires 7-15-89

OR

COUNTY CLERK, BEXAR COUNTY TEXAS

BY ______________________ DEPUTY

NOTE: A CERTIFICATE EXECUTED AND ACKNOWLEDGED BY AN ATTORNEY-IN-FACT SHALL INCLUDE A STATEMENT THAT THE ATTORNEY-IN-FACT HAS BEEN DULY AUTHORIZED IN WRITING BY HIS PRINCIPAL TO EXECUTE AND ACKNOWLEDGE THE SAME.

```
CASE NUMBER 89DA3322 displayed successfully
BEXAR COUNTYICE INFO CRIMINAL JUSTICE INFORMATION SYSTEM        02/22/1994
      TEXAS                        CASE PAGE                      14:21:32
__________________________________________________________________________

    COURT      CASE NUMBER     DEFENDANT NAME                        DATE OF
    D118       23DD1322        SMITH, JOHN                             BIRTH
                                                                  09/16/1943
    OFFENSE DESCRIPTION                               SEX: MALE
    12/15/1983 DEL HYDROMORPHONE UNDER 28 G           RACE: BLACK
    LOCATION: TEXAS DEPARTMENT OF CORRECTIONS
    LAST SETTING:                                 GRAND JURY: 05/12/1984 INDICTED
    CASE STATUS : 01/29/1987 SENTENCED
    DISPOSITION : 10/26/1984 PG CT-GUILTY
    JUDGEMENT   : 01/29/1987 SENTENCE-TERM
                                                 BOND: RWB 01/05/1986 999999.99
    START: 09/17/1986   END:                            BY:
    DEFENSE ATTORNEYS          BAR NUMBER                    YRS MO DY HRS
    JOHN H. DOE                2132123                  TERM: 8
                                                        FINE:
                                                  COURT COST:     284.50

    Enter-PF1--PF2--PF3--PF4--PF5--PF6--PF7--PF8--PF9--PF10--PF11--PF12--
          help retrn main
```

A search of the Federal Criminal Records can be conducted by going to the Federal Building, which are usually located in larger cities and cover a specific geographic area of the state. A name search can be done through a computer terminal provided for the public and is free of charge. The records will give any information on the subject which includes the charge, date of arrest, case status, personal information, and additional material. You can also ask the clerk to see the records.

The Federal Civil Records can be reviewed at the Federal courthouse. A name search will provide any lawsuits against the subject or company, the type of case, personal information, and other useful data. Federal civil cases typically involve cases filed against or by the government and may involve environmental violations, trade violations, and similar cases.

Depending on the nature of your investigation and whether or not it is a business, you may consider checking the Secretary of State's Records. This office is located in the capitol city of the state and can be accessed through a telephone call to a clerk. A name search can be conducted which will reveal whether or not the company has incorporated in that state, when it incorporated, who the officers, owners and registered agents are, addresses, and whether or not the company is in good standing with the state.

The State Comptroller's Office can be contacted and is located in the capitol city of the state. A clerk will check the records over the telephone, free of charge. The records can be searched by the person's name or the business name. The records will reflect if the subject is paying taxes due to owning a company, a franchise, having an oil or gas well, hotel, mining operation, truck company, or has inherited any money or property.

At the completion of your search of these records, you should have a better understanding of the subject in question. Each piece of information, when combined with the rest, will provide a full picture. An understanding of the person's general character, economic abilities, debts, complaints, and life style can be obtained.

Secretary of State Offices

ALABAMA
Office of Secretary of State
Corporations Division
State Office Building, Room 524
Montgomery, Alabama 36130

ALASKA
Division of Banking, Securities, Small Loans & Corporations
Pouch D
Juneau, Alaska 99811

ARIZONA
Arizona Corporation Commission
Secretary of State
1200 W. Washington
Phoenix, Arizona 85005

ARKANSAS
Secretary of State, Corporation Division
State Capitol
Little Rock, Arkansas 72201

CALIFORNIA
Secretary of State, Corporation Division
1230 J Street
Sacramento, California 95814

COLORADO
Department of State, Corporation Section
1560 Broadway, Suite 200
Denver, Colorado 80202

CONNECTICUT
Secretary of State, Corporation Division
30 Trinity St.
Hartford, Connecticut 06106

DELAWARE
Secretary of State, Corporation Division
P. O. Box 898
Dover, Delaware 19901

DISTRICT OF COLUMBIA
Recorder of Deeds
Recorder of Deeds Building
6th & D Street N.W.
Washington, D. C. 20001

FLORIDA
Secretary of State, Corporation Division
P. O. Box 6327
Tallahassee, Florida 32301

GEORGIA
Secretary of State, Corporation Division
#2 Martin Luther King Jr. Dr., S. E.
Atlanta, Georgia 30034

HAWAII
Department of Regulatory Agencies Corporations
1010 Richards St.
Honolulu, Hawaii 96813

IDAHO
Secretary of State, Corporation Division
State House
Boise, Idaho 83720

ILLINOIS
Secretary of State, Corporation Division
Centennial Building, Room 328
Springfield, Illinois 62756

INDIANA
Secretary of State, Corporation Division
State House, Room 155
Indianapolis, Indiana 46204

IOWA
Secretary of State, Corporation Division
East 14th & Walnut St.
Des Moines, Iowa 50319

KANSAS
Secretary of State, Corporation Division
State House, Room 200
Topeka, Kansas 66612

KENTUCKY
Secretary of State, Corporation Division
Capitol Building
Frankfort, Kentucky 40601

LOUISIANA
Department of State, Corporation Division
P. O. Box 44125
Baton Rouge, Louisiana 70804

MAINE
Secretary of State, Corporation Division
State House, Station 101
Augusta, Maine 04333

MARYLAND
Department of Assessments and Taxations
Corporation Division
301 W. Preston St.
Baltimore, Maryland 21201

MASSACHUSETTS
Secretary of the Commonwealth
Corporations Division
One Ashburton Place, Room 1713
Boston, Massachusetts 02108

MICHIGAN
Department of Commerce, Corporate Division
6546 Mercantile Dr.
Lansing, Michigan 48909

MINNESOTA
Secretary of State, Corporation Division
State Office Building, Room 180
St. Paul, Minnesota 55155

MISSISSIPPI
Secretary of State, Corporation Division
P. O. Box 136
Jackson, Mississippi 39205

MISSOURI
Secretary of State, Corporation Division
P. O. Box 1159
Jefferson City, Missouri 65102

MONTANA
Secretary of State, Corporation Division
State Capitol, Room 202
Helena, Montana 59620

NEBRASKA
Secretary of State, Corporation Division
The Capitol Building
Lincoln, Nebraska 68509

NEVADA
Secretary of State, Corporation Division
Capitol Complex
Carson City, Nevada 89710

NEW HAMPSHIRE
Secretary of State, Corporation Dept.
State House Annex, Room 204
Concord, New Hampshire 03301

NEW JERSEY
Secretary of State, Corporations
State House, CN 308
Trenton, New Jersey 08625

NEW MEXICO
Secretary of State, State Corporations
Post Office Box Drawer 1269
Sante Fe, New Mexico 87504

NEW YORK
Dept. of State, Division of Corporations
162 Washington Ave.
Albany, New York 12231

NORTH CAROLINA
Secretary of State, Corporation Division
300 North Salisbury Street
Raleigh, North Carolina 27611

OHIO
Secretary of State, Corporation Division
50 East Broad Street
Columbus, Ohio 43215

OKLAHOMA
Secretary of State, Corporation Division
State Capitol Building, Room 101
Oklahoma City, Oklahoma 73105

OREGON
Dept. of Commerce, Corporation Division
158 12th Street, N.E.
Salem, Oregon 97301

PENNSYLVANIA
Secretary of State, Corporation Division
North Office Building, Room 308
Harrisburg, Pennsylvania 17120

PUERTO RICO
Corporation Division
Commonwealth of Puerto Rico
Fortaleza Street, #50
San Juan, Puerto Rico 00904

RHODE ISLAND
Secretary of State, Corporation Division
270 Westminster Mall
Providence, Rhode Island 02903

SOUTH CAROLINA
Secretary of State, Corporation Division
Wade Hampton Office Building
Columbia, South Carolina 29204

TENNESSEE
Secretary of State, Corporate Section
James K. Polk Building, Room 500
Nashville, Tennessee 37219

TEXAS
Secretary of State, Corporations Section
P. O. Box 13697
Austin, Texas 78711

UTAH
Secretary of State, Corporations
160 East Third Street
Salt Lake City, Utah 84110

VERMONT
Secretary of State, Corporations
109 State Street, Pavilion Building
Montpelier, Vermont 05602

VIRGIN ISLANDS
Corporation Division
Territory of Virgin Islands
Charlette Amalie, St. Thomas
Virgin Islands 00801

VIRGINIA
Secretary of State, State Corporations
Post Office Box 1197
Richmond, Virginia 23209

WASHINGTON
Secretary of State, Corporations
211 12th Street
Olympia, Washington 98504

WEST VIRGINIA
Secretary of State, Corporations
State Capitol Building
Charleston, West Virginia 25305

WISCONSIN
Secretary of State, Corporations
P. O. Box 7648
Madison, Wisconsin 53707

WYOMING
Secretary of State, Corporation Section
110 Capitol Building
Cheyenne, Wyoming 82002

CHAPTER EIGHT

CIVIL RECORDS

The civil records can be a wealth of useful information which can lead to other searches. It is not uncommon for cases such as divorces to have a list of all of the debts and property owned, which may include a ranch or condominium in other areas of the country. The reason for searching the records will have an impact on the information that you pay specific attention to. If you are trying to locate a person, you will pay more attention to employment information, the names of relatives, addresses, etc. If you are trying to locate hidden assets, you will pay more attention to property listings and similar information. However, any of the information may be the one break you were looking for to make the whole picture come together.

The Scam Artist: I was contacted by an attorney from a different city who needed help locating a subject so that he could have a notice to appear in court citation (subpoena) served on a subject. The client indicated the subject had property in San Antonio and felt that it was a good place to start. He further stated that the subject had "scammed his client" out of a large sum of money which they hoped to regain. Before the investigation was completed, I had searched records by telephone, mail, and computer on three different continents and in a fifth of the states in the U. S. The subject was found to have been running several scams at one time which included U. S. investors in an oil drilling deal in Australia. Due to the pressure of investors, the subject was forced to actually drill, so that the investors could see something occurring. Through this and other scams, I found that the subject owned several aircraft's which he flew around the world in. However, I eventually determined that the subject had relatives in Tennessee and through the assistance of the neighbors and the local police, found out when the subject was there and had the citation served on the subject.

To determine whether a subject has been involved in any lawsuits, either by suing someone, or having someone sue them, you should start with the County's District Civil Records. If a search reveals that the person has property in another county or state, a search should obviously be conducted in that area as well. In divorce cases, you will have information on the children that start with their names, which may be different and will provide new search possibilities. If one of the parties is seeking child support or has filed for contempt of court due to non-payment of child support, useful information can be obtained. The party will normally have to list clothing expenses (with department stores listed), medical expenses (with the doctors listed), school expenses with the receipts, and extra-curricular activity expenses (music lessons, karate, etc.). First of all, you will get a better understanding of their activities. Secondly, you will determine what the person's general budget is, the class of stores they shop at, the class of clothing and household goods they buy and other interesting information.

If the civil case involves a bad debt, the file will reflect whether or not the debt has not been paid due to a lack of money. It is not uncommon for a lawsuit to be filed against a person who refused to pay for a product which was a "lemon". For example, if a person bought a car and it had problems that the dealer could not or refused to correct, the person may have retaliated by failing to pay for the car. Just because there is a "bad debt" case listed, does not necessarily mean the person is economically unstable. By reading the file, the reason for the unpaid debt may become clear.

An old civil case involving injuries from an accident 5 to 10 years ago may be worth looking into depending on the nature of your search. It is not uncommon for people who are filing suit against you or who are alleging injuries due to your negligence to have prior cases on file. Although you may have an insurance company representing you, don't assume that they are investigating the other party. Normally, just the opposite it true. The insurance adjuster's main concern is investigating the accident to confirm which party caused the accident. The majority of the subjects are never properly investigated to see what their history is like. Insurance is a business and like all businesses, they try to reduce costs. Proper investigating takes time and costs money which they are not eager to spend. Although insurance fraud is on the increase, proper investigating is not. This is due to natural disasters such as hurricanes, flooding, earthquakes, and fires which has drained the resources of the industry.

A case involving a prior accident will let you know if the person "suddenly stopped" for an unknown reason, just like in your situation. The file will reflect whether or not the same doctors and lawyers are involved, if the same injuries are being alleged, and hopefully the amount of the settlement. Particular attention should be given to the type of vehicles involved and the damages to determine if this is a "crash car" which is used over and over to stage different accidents. In addition, doctor's reports will provide information of the subject's activities and life styles, pre-existing injuries, and often times indications of alcohol or substance abuse.

The County's Civil Records should be researched to determine any cases involving delinquent debts, unpaid taxes, divorces, child support, personal injury cases, and other general cases. Again, remember that the records are provided in two places. The county's district civil records are the more serious cases and usually involve damages over $1,000. These records are located in the district court clerk's office which is usually located in the courthouse. The county clerk's office maintains the county civil records. These records can be searched by name, or case number if you know one. The material will indicate the case number, the parties involved, the type of case, and the date it was filed. You can then ask the clerk to pull the file on that particular case. In the file, you may find personal information, debts, employers, relatives, amount of child support, vehicle information, and other related data.

The County Deed Records is a good source of information. The records are located in the county clerk's office in the courthouse. These records will provide information on lawsuits from other counties or states. Creditors who file liens against property and assets held by a subject may be reflected in these records as well as other civil litigation information. It is common for a name search to reveal records filed by law enforcement agencies in other counties against the subject. If the subject was convicted of criminal charges in another county or state, the judge may have filed a lien on property owned by a subject in the county they live in to ensure that court costs, damages, and other expenses are repaid.

Depending on the information you are searching for, the Federal Bankruptcy Court records may be researched. This is a type of law suit filed to keep creditors at bay and give the subject time to re-organize their financial abilities. Most courts have a telephone number which can be dialed and a message will guide you through a name search using the keypad to type in the person's name. You will find the case number, dates involved, persons involved, attorneys, and other pertinent information provided. You should then go to the court and review the file to determine personal information, properties, stocks, art, vessels, and other useful information.

A review of the Federal Civil Records should also be made to complete the picture. By doing a name search you can determine any lawsuits against the subject or company, the type of case, personal information, and other useful data. This can be reviewed at the Federal building. These Federal civil cases typically involve local cases filed against or by the government and may involve environmental violations, trade violations, and other similar federal violations.

CHAPTER NINE

CRIMINAL RECORDS

Too Good To Be True: I received a call from a client requesting my assistance in conducting a background investigation in reference to a new executive vice-president for the client. After hiring the subject and having worked two weeks, the client came to the conclusion that the subject's credentials may not be correct. I began to research the general records outlined in this book and quickly concluded that the information on the subject's resume and job application were the product of a vivid imagination. While trying to confirm the subject's education, I found that the subject had attended the university as stated, but never graduated (much less with honors). The job application had a two year gap in the subject's employment which was explained as being a time in which the subject explored other possible business interests. These "business interests" involved the subject having embezzled more than $130,000 from a prior employer. The two year "gap" in the employment records was due to the subject being in prison for embezzlement.

The fastest and easiest way to check a person's criminal history is through the use of the N.C.I.C. computer, used by law enforcement officials. Unfortunately, only law enforcement officials can legally obtain the information and the FBI (who oversees the data) has made an increased effort to determine and prosecute those officers who mishandle this material. Although this is the most complete data available, it often times leaves out some criminal records. Each law enforcement agency is required to report this information to the FBI, however, due to a lack of personnel and proper record keeping, some records never make it to the data base.

The same records can be obtained, but it requires more effort and time. Fortunately, this effort usually provides more complete data than the N.C.I.C. material anyway. First, check the county's district criminal records. These records are housed in the district court clerk's office, where a computer terminal is available to the public and no fee is generally charged. Secondly, check the county's criminal records and these can be checked at the county clerk's office again using a public access computer terminal at no charge. These records include the arrest information, the charge itself, make reference to police department records and often times provide other useful information such as relatives and employers.

Next, check the Federal Criminal Records. A search of these records can be conducted by going to the Federal building which is located in larger cities and covers a specific geographic area of the state. A name search can be done through a computer terminal provided for the public and is free of charge. These records will give any information on the subject which includes the charge, date of arrest, case status, personal information, and additional material. You can also ask the clerk for the file for your review, and possibly gain much more information.

The local police department's Municipal Court records should be searched if it is available to the public. Some have been removed from public access in recent years and a check of local policy should be made. A search by name can reveal any tickets issued to the subject. You should insist on reviewing the ticket itself. On the ticket, you will be provided the reason for the ticket, the location in which they were given the ticket, the person's address, date of birth, the vehicle and license plate numbers, their drivers license number, and sometimes their employer and social security number is also available.

A Police Department Survey should be conducted. These are available in most larger cities, and requires a fee (usually $5.00 to $25.00). This can be done by calling the police department and confirming that they provide this service, as well as the cost. You can then mail the request and money, or do so in person. A survey can be done by name and/or address. You typically have to specify which year(s) that are to be searched. The department may charge a separate fee per year and only the most current is normally necessary for locating someone anyway. A survey will provide you with every police call made associated with the subject's name or address in question. You will be able to identify the date of birth, date and time of the call, location, reason for the call, officers involved, and additional information.

The police department's "warrant desk" is a good source of information. Many police departments will advise the caller whether the subject has an outstanding warrant against them for failure to appear in court to answer criminal charges. Police department policies differ, but most want the person to know there is an outstanding warrant, hoping they will come into the police department on their own and take care of the matter.

The County Deed Records, which are located in the county clerk's office in the courthouse should be reviewed. It is common for a name search to reveal records filed by law enforcement agencies in other counties against the subject in question. If the subject was convicted of criminal charges in another county or state, the judge may have filed a lien on property owned by a subject in the county they live to ensure that damages, court cost, or other expenses are repaid.

CHAPTER TEN

Introduction of Pre-text

After you complete the record searches, you have to analyze what you have learned. It may be that you are still not satisfied or you need to confirm some of the information gathered. Or, it may be that virtually no information was obtained and you therefore have not satisfied your goal through the record searches. It may be necessary to contact some of the parties associated with the subject or people who may possibly know the person.

I can't over-emphasize the need to be careful in this area. While it is improbable that anyone will know that you searched the records discussed, you create new hazards once you begin talking to other people. The questions that need to be answered before you proceed with contacting other subjects include:

Is there a need? Do I really think any information learned in this manner will significantly alter the other information or facts already obtained?

Is what I hope to learn worth the possibility of the person finding out that someone is investigating them?

If the person you are investigating finds out you are investigating them, what are the anticipated risks and responses?

Should you make contact with these sources in person or by telephone? If the conversation does not go the way you anticipated, you can always hang up if you have called them. However, some people prefer to talk to other people face-to-face and may be more likely to talk to you in person.

You should anticipate the possibility of one of the sources becoming agitated by your inquiry. How would you handle this?

How should you approach the conversation? Should you use a pre-text or direct line of questioning?

Recognize that it takes PI's years of developing interviewing skills, people skills, and instincts that enable this type of investigation to be carried out successfully.

Once these and other questions have been answered and the need to contact other possible sources has been accessed, proceed with caution.

The Use of a Pre-text

Part of acquiring information is knowing how to utilize a "pre-text" line of questioning. A good PI knows that some people will give you information, but refuse to if they are identified or if they are giving it to the police. These types of people also place PI's in the same category as police. Therefore, certain methods have to be utilized to place the person at ease and make them comfortable about talking with you. A technique of "mis-direction" may therefore be required to complete the task.

For example, if you have obtained information that your subject may be living at a new address but are unsure if they are the same subject, you may want to call some of their neighbors. Through the record searches previously outlined, you have a list of neighbors but do not want to scare the subject into moving again if he finds out that someone is searching for them. Depending on your reason for finding a person, you may need to "mis-direct" the neighbors. You can call the neighbors and advise them that you work for a collection agency and are trying to locate a subject that has failed to pay one of your customer's accounts. You can then ask them if they know the subject in question who lives nearby the neighbor. You may be able to determine that the subject did recently move in, what the subject looks like, etc. Once you receive the information, you can then advise the neighbor that the subject living by them apparently is a different subject than the one you are looking for. This allows you to accomplish your goal, you put the neighbor at ease, and they probably won't tell the subject since you advised them it was not the same person. **NOTE:** Due to a new device recently on the market, some areas of the country now have the ability to determine the telephone number of someone calling their house. This is called "caller I.D." and a box is connected to the telephone which displays the number calling their home. The use of telephone "Pre-Text" methods should be discouraged in these areas.

Other Pre-Text lines of questioning should be conducted as the need arises and depending on the person and the situation to be addressed. The idea is to simply provide as little information as possible that could get back to the subject being investigated. If it does not matter if the person knows, a direct line of questioning may be utilized. Again, you have to assess the person, office, or company you will be talking with and determine how honest they are likely to be with you.

A pre-text or direct line of questioning may be useful in several situations. Assuming that you searched the records suggested and obtained information from the records, you may wish to contact neighbors, employers, or former employers. You should remember that a rapport has to be established between you and the person you talk with. They have no requirements to talk to you or answer any questions and you should therefore be courteous and cooperative. In addition, you should be careful not to say anything that would be considered as derogative, slanderous, or harassment. Another thought to remember is that employers of government agencies are probably over-worked and under-paid. You should, therefore, acknowledge the fact that they are busy and that you appreciate any assistance that they can give you.

Some of the possible sources that you may need to contact upon completion of the record searches include the following:

Neighbors — A list can be obtained by checking the city Criss-Cross, Polk's City Directory, or County Appraisal District. Former neighbors may also be a good source.

Real Estate Agents — If a person has placed their house on the market, or if they live in a rental property, contact with the real estate agent or home owner may be beneficial.

Apartment Leasing Agents — These people are usually good sources of information concerning the people who rent their property.

Employers — It is best to contact "former employers" as they are more likely to talk to you since they no longer have the person employed. Secondly, you do not want to interfere with the subject's employment abilities as you may face a law suit. Third, due to recent cases of stalking, employers are becoming more restrictive in the information released on their employees. In addition, most companies strictly enforce laws and/or policies concerning the release of information.

Police Officers/Sheriff's Deputies — A trip to the local police department or sheriff's department may be useful. You should enter the department and talk with any officer you see, or request to see one if there is not one immediately at hand. If the officer believes that your motive is pure and you pose no threat to the subject in question, they may provide you with their personal knowledge of the subject.

Probation Officer — If you have determined that the subject is or was on probation, hopefully, you also determined the probation officer's name. The officer's job is to keep up with the subject, his activities, present address, and employer. The probation officers are always over-worked and have very little time for this type of inquiry. However, depending on the officer, they may still be of assistance.

EMS — If a person was known to be in an accident or needed the Emergency Medical Services (ambulance), you may be able to obtain a copy of part of their records. If you determine which personnel made the call, you may be able to contact them and obtain useful information.

CHAPTER ELEVEN

SURVEILLANCE

Surveillance is an acquired skill which should only be considered by an individual as a last resort. Due to the recent increase in stalking cases, many states are passing anti-stalking laws designed to protect a subject from harassment and injury. You should therefore determine what laws may apply to your state regarding stalking prior to considering this method of investigation.

The increase of thefts, burglaries, drive-by shootings, and other crimes, has caused many neighbors to ban together for self-protection. It is not uncommon for neighbors to call the police on PI's conducting surveillance in their neighborhood. For PI's, this does not normally create a problem because they have the appropriate credentials to show the police and they should be sitting far enough away from the subject's house to prevent the person from seeing the police arrive. An individual who is checked by the police in reference to their being a "suspicious person", could create several problems. Although it is not unlawful to park in your car on a public street or parking lot, you should be aware of the laws governing parking, to prevent any tickets. (Ex: Parked facing the wrong direction, too close to a fire hydrant or intersection). If nothing else, the officer may be concerned about your motives and increase the patrols in that area.

A person should also consider the possibility of their parking and setting up surveillance down the street from the subject, but in front of one of their relative's or friend's houses. What are the problems associated with one of these people and eventually the subject himself knowing about the surveillance?

Before surveillance is initiated, the area of surveillance should be reviewed to determine the crime rate and chance for injury due to the type of neighborhood. If drug traffic is heavy in the area, the chance of you blending in and being unnoticed is slim due to the drug dealers having "spotters" who watch for police or unknown subjects. In addition, gangs go hand-in-hand with drug traffic and the possibility of sudden violence or drive-by shooting dramatically increases in these areas.

A good PI has specially equipped vehicles designed for surveillance, as well as long range cameras and video lenses which dramatically decrease the chances of detection. In addition, many PI's were former police officers who know the city, the streets, and the dangerous areas of town. Professional PI's have learned the art and skill of surveillance and are capable of driving in harsh road conditions, watching traffic and traffic laws, taking notes, and keeping up with the subject at the same time. The person who is being followed generally knows where they are headed, while the person conducting surveillance doesn't, which makes the job more difficult.

I remember a case in which I went out on for the first time and had never seen the subject or the house. A city park was situated on a hill over-looking the subject's house and offered great concealment. After just getting set up, I observed one of the four male subjects working on the car stop and enter the house. When I looked back at the door, I saw this subject looking at me through a rifle scope (with the rifle)! You never know how suspicious a person may be even though you have not given them cause.

The next consideration should be the reason for surveillance. Is surveillance being conducted just for the "excitement"? If so, the excitement of surveillance will quickly turn into boredom and unfulfilled expectations. Unlike T.V. shows, surveillance is usually conducted when it's too hot or too cold, raining, or in other harsh weather conditions and takes hours and hours of just sitting. A person conducting surveillance has to continually stare at the house and vehicles in question because any good investigator can tell you stories of how the subject slipped away when they took their eyes off the house to pour a cup of coffee. Nothing can describe the feelings that occur when you have spent hours and hours on surveillance and when the subject becomes active, you are nowhere around. The reason for the surveillance and the information you hope to acquire is a major consideration in deciding whether or not to conduct surveillance. In addition, a person must examine what they intend to do with the information obtained from the surveillance. For example, emotions run high in relationships in which one party believes that the other is being unfaithful. The spouse obviously knows the type of vehicle their spouse drives, as well as those of their spouses friends. Getting close enough to conduct surveillance in this situation will be the first obstacle. Next, what if your suspicions are confirmed? What type of reaction do you anticipate, can you control your emotions, and how will you use the information?

Obviously, because of the situations already discussed, as well as other factors, surveillance should be discouraged by the average person. General surveillance techniques evolve moment by moment depending on the situations, changes in geographic area/streets/neighborhoods, and other factors. Therefore, "teaching" someone to conduct surveillance would take a tremendous amount of explanation. Due to the risks involved and the average person's lack of experience in this area, it is anticipated that most people who utilize the information in this book will never need or desire to engage in surveillance. Therefore, no additional time will be allotted to this topic at this time.

CHAPTER TWELVE

Credit Reports

A person's credit and financial history is a part of their life which is considered off limits and secretive. The information is therefore maintained by only 2-3 major credit bureaus, who add, delete, and provide the information to creditors. Because of the nature of the information, the law prohibits anyone from having access to the information unless they have a written authorization from the person whose credit is to be checked. Although PI's have the ability to check credit reports, they are not allowed to do so without a signed authorization.

For the average person, checking another person's credit report is virtually impossible due to the legal issue. A person should be aware that creditors often incorrectly check a person's credit history due to similar names, zip codes, and social security numbers. Every person should check their own credit report at least once a year to review the information and make sure it's correct and to see who has been checking their credit. The local credit company (Ex: San Antonio Retail Merchants

Association) should be written and a request made for a copy of your credit history. Most companies allow a person to obtain a free copy of their own credit report each year.

If your goal is to determine the person's financial status, this can be done legally and with a minimal amount of time. First, check the *Bankruptcy Court Records* which are found in the federal building. These are located in the capitol city of the state and some state's have more than one office depending on the size and number of cases. You can access the records often time by a telephone number which allows you to punch in the person's name using the telephone key pad. The case number, persons involved, date it was filed, and the attorney will commonly be provided. You can then go down to the office or write for a copy of the file for your review. The information contains the financial records, property, assets, stocks, bonds, and any other pertinent information about the subject. Contact with the attorney and/or the creditors can provide a clearer picture of the person's finances.

The *County Deed Records* will be another good place to search due to the files indicating information on property being sold or transferred, inheritances, tax liens, judgements, and other various records. These records are usually found in the county clerk's office at the courthouse and are free to search.

The *County Financing Statements* are records filed to protect a bank or creditor when they make a loan to a business. They will list any collateral which belongs to the business and any lienholders. The records are also found in the county clerk's office in the courthouse and are free to access.

The *County Appraisal District* records are usually located in or near the courthouse. A name search can be conducted free of charge and will provide any property owned by the subject in that county. The mortgage company and appropriate addresses will usually be shown in the records as well.

The *County Tax Assessors* office, which is located normally in the courthouse, is a good source to check. The records will list any taxes owed by an individual or company. A company will have to pay taxes on assets such as office equipment even if they do not own the building they are in.

The *County Assumed Name* records is located in the county clerk's office in the courthouse and is free to access by the public. The records can be searched by name and will list any businesses or names that the subject may be doing business as.

The *County District Civil* records, which is located in the county district clerk's office in the courthouse and the county civil records which is located in the county clerk's office are worth researching. Both can be searched in person, by mail, and generally by telephone. The records may provide information as to the property owned by the subject if there is a divorce case, bad debt case, or other related cases on file. If a case if located, ask the clerk to review the file to better determine any useful information.

The *State Department of Parks and Wildlife* is a source to check and is usually done over the telephone. The clerk can tell you if the subject has any boats or other vessels listed in their name and the information on the vessel.

The *State Comptroller's* office monitors and collects taxes owed to the state from businesses and individuals. Their office can be called and a name search can generally be conducted over the telephone. The office is normally found in the capitol city of the state. Records pertaining to oil wells, inheritances, businesses and other interesting information may be found.

For conducting a more complete investigation of this nature, please refer to Chapter Six on hidden assets investigations. However, this brief outline will provide some of the general information and searches that can be conducted instead of a credit check if you do not have the proper written authorization or methods in which to conduct the search yourself.

CHAPTER THIRTEEN

Child Support Investigations

Although the government, state and counties, all have offices designed to track down for free ex-spouses who owe child support and alimony, the results are often not satisfactory to some. Unfortunately, like all government agencies, their work load is too heavy and the searches may take too long. In addition, their method of searching also involves contacting other government agencies which have the same problems. A new industry has recently been created to assist in the ex-spouse search. These businesses will assist in locating the subject in return for a percentage of the monies collected or for an up front fee.

The reality of this situation is that a large majority of families depend on this support from ex-spouses. The family often becomes frustrated by the slow moving searches conducted by government agencies and do not have the money for child support search agencies. The fact is, the government agencies want to help, they just don't have the ability to handle the workload.

Once the subject is found or someone gives them information on the subject's whereabouts, the agencies move quickly.

For those interested in speeding up the process, the following information will help you locate your former spouse. However, two questions need to be addressed. First, do you intend to approach the ex-spouse yourself or turn the information over to the appropriate agency? Depending on the answer to the preceding question, you may or may not want the ex-spouse to know you are looking for them. Typically, if you intend to turn the information over to the appropriate agency, you do not want the subject to know he is being sought after or they may move and disappear again. However, if the person is the type that can be reasoned with and who normally will pay the child support if approached, it may not matter if they know about the investigation. We will therefore discuss both situations and how to proceed accordingly.

The following records should be researched regardless of whether or not it matters if the subject knows they are being investigated. These records can be searched without anyone becoming aware of the search being conducted.

First, check the last known location where the subject was known to be. Check with the directory assistance in that area to see if the person is listed as having a telephone number in their name. Even if the operator indicates that the number is unlisted, you at least know that the subject is still in that area. Remember to check for listings using the subject's initials, middle name, maiden name, divorcee names, girlfriends/boyfriends, and relatives if you know their names.

Next, if you are relatively sure that the subject has moved out of the area, check directory assistance in other locations. For example, if the subject has family in other states or was born somewhere else, check these areas. Also check the areas where the ex-spouse went to college, was stationed while in the military, or any place the subject ever talked about wanting to live.

If you know of a former address, contact the Post Office and check for a forwarding address. This can be done by mail or in person, but you must fill out the post office's form and submit $3.00. This can be done regardless of where the old address is. You simply have to make the request through the post office which handles the address in question. To do this, call any post office and they can provide you with the address and telephone number for the appropriate post office station. Request the change of address form under the "Freedom of Information Act", section 352.643, of the Administrative Support Manual. If you receive an updated address, conduct the same search using the new address. Although the post office can provide you with the most recent address, it is not uncommon for the check to only provide the initial change of address. Before doing this, however, you may want to check with directory assistance and some of the following records to verify the information.

If none of the searches provide any useful information, contact the public utilities in your area or the area the subject may be living in. Each public utility department has different policies about releasing this information. However, all allow the customer to complete a form restricting anyone from getting information on their particular account. The utility departments often release the account information since the person can restrict the material if they so choose to do so. A search is typically done by name, suspected address, or social security number. You may be able to do this over the telephone or the department may require a written request.

A check with Voter's Registration is an easy search and will provide an address, telephone number, and sometimes the employer. Depending on the type of person, they may or may not register to vote. It is not uncommon for a subject to register to vote just to satisfy the residency requirements for some jobs and government programs. The voter's registration office is located in or near the county courthouse and a search is usually done free of charge. The records can be accessed by name or social security number. The information is the most current right before and right after a major election.

The Appraisal District records for the county should be researched to see if the subject has any property which they own. Again, check the areas the ex-spouse may have talked about or had prior interests in because they may have purchased land there anticipating that they would build a house on it. If this is the case, the person may be living in a travel trailer or mobile home on the land until the house is built. The appraisal district records are searched by name or address and give the current and former owner of the property. While searching, be sure to search for relatives and friends who the subject may be living with.

The County Deed records are another good source of information. Typically, the records list property "deeds" associated with buying or selling property. However, other records are also included in these areas of the records. They include liens filed against the person or property due to unpaid taxes, court costs, judgements, or other types of records. Any inheritances are usually listed here and property willed to the subject may be the location in which they are residing. If a power of attorney is listed which gives a person the legal right to act on their behalf, you may determine relatives or an attorney who is handling the subject's affairs. Some people who want to hide, hire an attorney to act as a shield between themselves and others, such as creditors. If the power of attorney was given to a relative, friend, or attorney, it will be a source of contact and can be useful information. Other records listed here will be guardianship orders, child support orders, garnishment orders, and other tools which may lead you to the ex-spouse. The deed records are usually part of the county clerk's office which is located in the courthouse and are free to review.

The County Tax records are a good source to check because taxes have to be paid on any property or assets owned by a person or company. Although the appraisal district records should have told you if the subject owns property, it doesn't hurt to cross-check the information. In addition, companies who do not own their office space still have to pay taxes on office furniture, equipment, and other assets. These taxes will be listed in the records which are located in the county clerk's office inside most courthouses and there are generally no fees to search the records.

The County Clerk's office also houses the assumed name records for the county. A company who operates in the county has to file an assumed name record listing the owners and the addresses. In addition, individuals who change their names also file an assumed name record. The searches are usually free to the public and are a good source of information.

The county's civil record should be checked to see if the ex-spouse has filed a lawsuit against anyone or if someone has filed a suit against them. If a case is found, the attorneys representing both parties will be shown and they can be contacted. If your lucky, the case is still pending and is set for trial in the near future. You may be able to catch up to the subject when they appear at court. Additionally, information in the file itself may be useful. If a case is found, ask the clerk to retrieve the file for your review. The records may indicate where the person was served with the notice of the lawsuit, an employer, relatives, and other pertinent information. Remember that there are the county civil records, which involve minor cases and the damages are typically less than $1,000. In addition, the county district records involve divorces, custody cases, damage cases, judgements, bad debts, and other cases which involve damages over $1,000. The county civil records are part of the county clerk's office while the district civil records are part of the district court clerk's records. Each can be searched free of charge at the courthouse by conducting a name search.

The county criminal records are also divided up according to the seriousness of the charge. The county clerk's office houses the county criminal records (misdemeanor cases under

$1,000 in damages) while the district court clerk house the district criminal records (misdemeanor and felony cases with damages over $1,000). A name search can be conducted at the courthouse and the actual file reviewed if a listing is found. The file will tell you the charge, date of the charge, trial date (which hopefully is pending) and where the arrest was made. The place of arrest may be important depending on the location. For example, if the subject was arrested at a bar, they probably frequent the establishment and live nearby. If the place of arrest was a house or an apartment, the subject may live there or may have been visiting friends who live there. If the person is on probation, the records will indicate this and the probation office may be a good source as they are required to keep in touch with the probationer.

In addition to these searches, refer to the information previously outlined in Chapter 2, "Locating People". If you are still at a dead-end, you may try to have mail forwarded to the subject through one of the following:

A. *The Social Security Administration* will forward letters or legal notices. Contact them at 6401 Security Blvd., Baltimore, Maryland 21235.

B. *The Department of Veterans Affairs,* Veterans Benefits Administration, Administrative Support Staff (20A52), 810 Vermont Ave., Northwest, Washington, D. C. 20420, will forward mail.

C. *The Salvation Army* will forward letters and can be contacted through local offices in the community.

D. *The Civil Air Patrol Locator Service* will assist in locating and forwarding mail to subjects who were a part of their organization and can be reached through Maxwell AFB, in Alabama.

E. *The U. S. Civil Service* will forward letters to current or former civil service employees. Contact their office at the U. S. Office of Personnel Management, 1900 East E. St., Washington, D. C. 20415.

F. *The U. S. Public Health Service* will forward mail to anyone who has ever been employed with their department. Contact them at the Dept. of Health and Human Services, 5600 Fishers Lane, Parklawn Building, Room 4-35, Rockville, Maryland 20857.

G. *The Railroad Retirement Board* will forward letters to those employed with a railroad. Contact them at the Railroad Retirement Board, 844 Rush St., Chicago, IL. 60611.

H. *The Department Of State, Passport Division,* may be a source of locating a subject if they were taken or left the country at any time as a U. S. Passport is required. Contact the Dept., c/o the Office of Freedom of Information, 2201 C Street, Northwest, Washington, D. C. 20520-1239.

I. *The U. S. Court of Military Appeals* and the U. S. Court of Veterans Appeals may be a source of information if a military person ever filed an appeal for various benefits or to contest findings. Both courts are located in Washington, D. C., and can be located through directory assistance.

J. *The U. S. Tax Court* hears cases of disputes under $10,000 involving the IRS and are located in Washington, D. C. If a search locates information, a current address is probable since the nature of the case involves money.

K. *The U. S. Claims Court* hears claims against the government and any search may reveal information on the subject if a match is found. The Court is located in Washington, D. C. and can easily be reached through directory assistance.

L. *The General Services Administration* in Washington, D. C., is responsible for awarding contracts to contractors who supply products and services to the government. If your subject has a business which may provide products or services to the government, you may receive current information on the subject through this search.

Child Support Agencies

ALABAMA
Child Support Enforcement Division
Dept. of Human Resources
64 N. Union St.
Montgomery, Al. 36130
(205) 242-2734

ALASKA
Child Support Enforcement Division
Dept. of Revenue
550 W. 7th Ave., 4th Floor
Anchorage, Alaska 99501
(907) 276-3441

ARIZONA
Child Support Enforcement
2222 W. Encanto
P.O. Box 6123
Phoenix, Arizona 85005
(602) 252-0236

ARKANSAS
Division of Child Support Enforcement
Arkansas Social Services
P.O. Box 3358
Little Rock, Arkansas 72203
(501) 682-8398

CALIFORNIA
Division of Child Program Management
Dept. of Social Service
744 P Street-Mail Stop 9-011
Sacramento, CA. 95814
(916) 322-8495

COLORADO
Division of Child Support Enforcement
Dept. of Social Services
1575 Sherman St.
Denver, Colorado 80203
(303) 866-5994

CONNECTICUT
Bureau of Child Support Enforcement
Dept. of Human Resources
1049 Asylum Ave.
Hartford, Connecticut 06105
(203) 566-3053

DELAWARE
Division of Child Support Enforcement
Dept. of Health & Social Services
P. O. Box 904
New Castle, Delaware 19720
(302) 421-8300

DISTRICT OF COLUMBIA
Office of Paternity & Child Support
425 I Street, N.W., Suite 3013
Washington, D.C. 20001
(202) 724-5610

FLORIDA
Office of Child Support Enforcement
Health and Rehabilitation Services
1317 Winewood Blvd., Building 3
Tallahassee, Florida 32399
(904) 488-9900

GEORGIA
Office of Child Support Recovery
State Dept. of Human Resources
878 Peachtree St. N.E., Suite 529
Atlanta, Georgia 30309
(404) 894-4119

GUAM
Office of Attorney General, Child Support
194 Hernan Cortez Ave.
Agana, Guam 96910
(671) 477-2036

HAWAII
Dept. of Attorney General, Child Support
P.O. Box 1860
Honolulu, Hawaii 96805
(808) 548-5779

IDAHO
Bureau of Child Support Enforcement
450 W. State St., Towers Building
Boise, Idaho 83720
(208) 334-5710

ILLINOIS
Division of Child Support Enforcement
201 S. Grand Ave. East, Bloom Building
Springfield, Illinois 62794
(217) 782-1366

INDIANA
Dept. of Public Welfare, Child Support
141 S. Meridian St.
Indianapolis, Indiana 46225
(317) 232-4885

IOWA
Bureau of Collections
Iowa Dept. of Human Services
Hoover Building-5th Floor
Des Moines, Iowa 50319
(515) 281-5580

KANSAS
Child Support Enforcement Program
300 S. West Oakley St.
P.O. Box 497
Topeka, Kansas 66603
(913) 296-3237

KENTUCKY
Division of Child Support Enforcement
Dept. of Social Insurance
275 E. Main St., 6th Floor East
Frankfort, Kentucky 40621
(502) 564-2285

LOUISIANA
Support Enforcement Division
Dept. of Social Services
P.O. Box 94065
Baton Rouge, Louisiana 70804
(504) 342-4780

MAINE
Support Enforcement and Location Unit
Dept. of Human Services
State House, Station 11
Augusta, Maine 04333
(207) 289-2886

MARYLAND
Dept. of Human Resources, Child Support
311 W. Saratoga St.
Baltimore, Maryland 21201
(301) 333-3979

MASSACHUSETTS
Dept. of Revenue, Child Support
Division
215 First St.
Cambridge, Massachusetts 02124
(617) 621-4200

MICHIGAN
Dept. of Social Services, Child Support
300 S. Capitol Ave., Suite 621
Lansing, Michigan 48909
(517) 373-7570

MINNESOTA
Dept. of Human Services, Child
Support
444 LaFayette Rd.
St. Paul, Minnesota 55155
(612) 296-2499

MISSISSIPPI
State Dept. of Public Welfare, Child
Support
515 E. Armite St.
Jackson, Mississippi 39205
(601) 354-0341

MISSOURI
Dept. of Social Services, Child Support
P.O. Box 1527
Jefferson City, Missouri 65102
(314) 751-4301

MONTANA
Dept. of Rehabilitation, Child Support
P.O. Box 5955
Helena, Montana 59604
(406) 444-4614

NEBRASKA
Dept. of Social Services, Child Support
P.O. Box 95026
Lincoln, Nebraska 68509
(402) 471-9125

NEVADA
Dept. of Human Resources, Child
Support
2527 N. Carson St.
Carson City, Nevada 89710
(702) 885-4744

NEW HAMPSHIRE
Division of Welfare, Child Support
Enforcement
6 Hazen Rd.
Concord, New Hampshire 03301
(603) 271-4426

NEW JERSEY
Dept. of Human Services, Child Support
CN 716
Trenton, New Jersey 08625
(609) 588-2401

NEW MEXICO
Dept. of Human Services, Child Support
P. O. Box 25109
Santa Fe, New Mexico 87504
(505) 827-7200

NEW YORK
Dept. of Social Services, Child Support
P. O. Box 14-1 Commerce Plaza
Albany, New York 12260
(518) 474-9081

NORTH DAKOTA
Dept. of Human Services, Child Support
State Capitol
Bismarch, North Dakota 58505

NORTH CAROLINA
Dept. of Human Services, Child Support
437 N. Harrington St.
Raleigh, North Carolina 27603
(919) 733-4120

OHIO
Dept. of Human Services, Child Support
30 E. Broad St.
Columbus, Ohio 43266
(614) 466-3233

OKLAHOMA
Dept. of Human Services, Child Support
P. O. Box 25352
Oklahoma City, Oklahoma 73125
(405) 424-5871

OREGON
Dept. of Human Resources, Child Support
P. O. Box 14506
Salem, Oregon 97309
(503) 378-5439

PENNSYLVANIA
Dept. of Public Welfare, Child Support
P. O. Box 8018
Harrisburg, Pennsylvania 17105
(717) 787-3672

PUERTO RICO
Dept. of Social Services, Child Support
Call Box 3349
San Juan, Puerto Rico 00904
(809) 722-4731

RHODE ISLAND
Dept. of Human Services, Family Support
77 Dorrance St.
Providence, Rhode Island 02903
(401) 277-2409

SOUTH CAROLINA
Dept. of Social Services, Child Support
P. O. Box 1520
Columbia, South Carolina 29202
(803) 737-5870

SOUTH DAKOTA
Dept. of Social Services, Child Support
700 Governors Dr.
Pierre, South Dakota 57501
(605) 773-3641

TENNESSEE
Dept. of Human Services, Child Support
400 Deadrick St.
Nashville, Tennessee 37219
(615) 741-1820

TEXAS
Attorney General's Office, Child Support
P.O. Box 12548
Austin, Texas 78711
(512) 463-2181

UTAH
Dept. of Social Services, Recovery Services
120 N. 200 West
Salt Lake City, Utah 84145
(801) 538-4400

VERMONT
Dept. of Social Welfare, Child Support
103 S. Main St.
Waterbury, Vermont 05676
(802) 241-2910

VIRGIN ISLANDS
Dept. of Law, Support & Paternity Division
46 Norre Gade
St. Thomas, Virgin Islands 00801
(809) 776-0372

VIRGINIA
Dept. of Social Services, Child Support
8007 Discovery Dr.
Richmond, Virginia 23288
(804) 662-9297

WASHINGTON
Dept. of Social & Health Services
Mail Stop HJ-31
Olympia, Washington 98504
(206) 586-6111

WEST VIRGINIA
Dept. of Social Services, Child Advocate Dept.
1900 Washington St., East
Charleston, West Virginia 25305
(304) 348-3780

WISCONSIN
Bureau of Child Support, Economic Support
1 West Wilson St., Room 382
Madison, Wisconsin 53707
(608) 266-1175

WYOMING
Division of Public Assistance, Child Support
Hathaway Building
Cheyenne, Wyoming 82002
(307) 777-7892

CHAPTER FOURTEEN

Workman's Compensation

Workman's Compensation was designed to provide benefits to an employee if they were injured while in the extent of their employment. Unfortunately, just like any other large program, a great deal of abuse has crept into the system.

The scenarios that occur in this type of fraud are endless. However, the injury usually occurs with no witnesses around, is commonly reported on Monday mornings, and attorneys may become involved almost immediately.

A person may want to research the records for workman's compensation injuries for a number of reasons. The most obvious is to determine if the subject appears to be abusing the system or to see if the prior injuries may affect their ability to perform other jobs. However, the records can reveal information about the person's general character and may assist in locating the individual.

First, contact the State Board which regulates Workman's Compensation in your State. You will probably have to do this in writing. A name search can be conducted and any information, such as the person's date of birth, social security number, and prior employers, should be enclosed. If a match is found, you will determine the dates, employer, type of injury, disability rating if applicable, the doctors, and the attorneys involved. You may then request a copy of the file itself to review. Although some states do not provide this information to the public, the majority do.

It is very common for an injury to be reported on a Monday. This occurs because the person may have been working in their yard, playing sports or engaging in other activities over the weekend. If a person turns in an injury on a Monday, a red flag should immediately go up to alert you of the possibility of fraud. Although the person may have insurance which will take care of their medical bills regardless of how they were injured, they may attempt to report it as a job related injury so that they can receive at least part of their payroll check while off of work. For those who really know the system, they may milk this into a large settlement.

I remember one case in which a person reported an injury on a Monday. The employer immediately became suspicious and an investigation was initiated. A search of the local police department's records revealed that the subject had been at a bar the Saturday night before and had gotten into a fight. A review of the report revealed that the subject reported the exact injuries he had reported as injuring on the job the Monday morning following the fight. A police department survey can be conducted through most police departments and usually costs $5 to $25.00. A name and/or address search can be conducted. This will let you know of any police calls associated with the subject's name or any calls made to the subject's residence. You may discover family disturbances, auto accidents or other incidents which occurred just prior to the date the person reported they were injured. Not all police departments offer this service. However, a check with the city police department and the sheriff's department should be made if they allow the public to access this information in your area.

I worked one case in which the subject was found to have a history of workman's compensation injuries. I conducted additional record searches and determined that the subject had a business on the side. Putting all of the picture together, it appeared relatively certain that the subject's recent injury was a possible fraud. The investigation concluded with video documentation of the subject being observed as he did odd jobs to collect cash, in addition to building a large two-story house on some property he owned.

It is not uncommon for people to file claims to coincide with their lifestyle. For instance, some people file claims around Thanksgiving and Christmas to allow them more opportunity to celebrate. Others may file a claim so that they can work at their own business while being paid for the workman's compensation injury. The subject may have a new boat and would like more time off to enjoy it. Whatever the reason, appropriate record checks can help eliminate this.

A check of the county civil records may reveal a wealth of information. For instance, if a divorce case is found, the subject may have to pay child support. If they are on workman's compensation, the benefits usually do not apply to child support and they may actually bring home more money by being on workman's compensation. These records are located in the courthouse and are in the county clerk's office and the district court clerk's office. You may find previous lawsuits against former employers for job related injuries. The file should be requested from the clerk and the type of injury, circumstances surrounding the injury, doctor's bills, and other information should be compared to any injury currently under investigation.

The county criminal records should also be researched and are located in the county courthouse just like the civil records. I remember investigating a subject who had been off work under workman's compensation for almost two years. The subject was found to be incarcerated in the county jail for almost one year. The additional investigation revealed the subject's wife had moved in with another man and was illegally cashing the checks. When conducting a search by name, I have discovered cases where the subject was arrested for assault just before the reported date of injury and later discovered that the fight caused the injury. The records may list theft charges and others as serious as murder. Whether or not the information assists in the defense of the workman's compensation claim or not, you may discover the person's true character. The records may reflect drug or alcohol abuse which may have contributed to the cause of the injury, domestic problems, or other informative facts. If a match is found, ask the clerk to allow you to review the file to better understand the facts.

The Assumed Name Records, located in the county clerk's office in the courthouse can be researched free of charge. The records will provide the name of any businesses the subject may own. This may be the reason that the subject wants to be off on workman's compensation benefits which will allow him to work at his own business.

The Secretary of State's Office and/or the State Comptroller's Office, which are both located in the capitol city of the state, may be another source to check. A name search can be done over the telephone and the clerk will advise you of any businesses or taxes being paid by businesses owned by the subject.

The County Appraisal District records should be reviewed to see if the person owns a lot of rental property. The subject may need time off to work on the houses. These records are usually located in or near the county courthouse and a name search can be conducted free of charge by the public in most cases.

Contacting the neighbors of the subject may be another source of determining the person's activities and you may learn that the person was actually injured working on a car or in some other manner. This method is generally not recommended, however, because there is a good possibility that the neighbor will tell the person that someone called about them. You may in fact, contact a neighbor who is a friend or relative and the subject will probably alter or stop any activity they had been involved in.

Workman's Compensation Offices

ALABAMA
Workmen's Compensation Division
Industrial Relation Building
Montgomery, Alabama 36130

ALASKA
Worker's Compensation
P. O. Box 25512
Juneau, Alaska 99802

ARIZONA
State Compensation Fund
3031 North Second Street
Phoenix, Arizona 85012

ARKANSAS
Workers' Compensation Commission
625 Marshall Street
Little Rock, Arkansas 72201

CALIFORNIA
State Compensation Insurance Fund
1275 Market Street
San Francisco, California 94103

COLORADO
Workers' Compensation Section
1313 Sherman Street, Room 314
Denver, Colorado 80203

CONNECTICUT
Workers' Compensation Commission
1890 Dixwell Avenue
Hamden, Connecticut 06514

DELAWARE
Industrial Accident Board
820 North French Street
Wilmington, Delaware 19801

DISTRICT OF COLUMBIA
Office of Workers' Compensation
Post Office Box 56098
Washington, D. C. 20011

LOUISIANA
Office of Workers' Compensation
Post Office Box 94040
Baton Rouge, Louisiana 70804

MAINE
Workers' Compensation Commission
State House, Room 27
Augusta, Maine 04333

MARYLAND
Workers' Compensation Commission
6 North Liberty Street
Baltimore, Maryland 21201

MASSACHUSETTS
Industrial Accident Board
600 Washington Street
Boston, Massachusetts 02111

MICHIGAN
Bureau of Workers' Disability
Post Office Box 30016
Lansing, Michigan 48909

MINNESOTA
Workers' Compensation Division
443 Layafayette Road
St. Paul, Minnesota 55155

MISSISSIPPI
Workers' Compensation Commission
Post Office Box 5300
Jackson, Mississippi 39216

MISSOURI
Division of Workers' Compensation
Post Office Box 58
Jefferson City, Missouri 65102

MONTANA
Division of Workers' Compensation
5 South Last Chance Gulch
Helena, Montana 59604

OKLAHOMA
Oklahoma Workers' Compensation
1915 North Stiles
Oklahoma City, Oklahoma 73105

OREGON
Dept. of Insurance & Finance
Labor and Industries Bldg.
Salem, Oregon 97310

PENNSYLVANIA
Workers' Compensation Bureau
1171 S. Cameron
Harrisburg, Pennsylvania 17104

PUERTO RICO
State Insurance Fund
GPO Box 5038
San Juan, Puerto Rico 00936

RHODE ISLAND
Dept. of Worker Compensation
610 Manton Ave.
Providence, Rhode Island 02909

SOUTH CAROLINA
Industrial Commission
1615 Marian Street
Columbia, South Carolina 29202

SOUTH DAKOTA
Dept. of Labor
700 Governors Drive
Pierre, South Dakota 57501

TENNESSEE
Workers' Compensation Dept.
501 Union Building
Nashville, Tennessee 37219

FLORIDA
Dept. of Workers' Compensation
1321 Executive Center Drive
Tallahassee, Florida 32399

GEORGIA
Dept. of Workers' Compensation
One CNN Center
Atlanta, Georgia 30303

HAWAII
Disability Compensation Division
830 Punchbowl Street
Honolulu, Hawaii 96813

IDAHO
Idaho Industrial Commission
317 Main Street
Boise, Idaho 83720

ILLINOIS
Illinois Industrial Commission
100 West Randolph
Chicago, Illinois 60611

INDIANA
Industrial Board
100 North Senate Avenue
Indianapolis, Indiana 46204

IOWA
Industrial Commissioner's Office
1000 East Grand Street
Des Moines, Iowa 50319

KANSAS
Division of Workers' Compensation
900 Jackson, Room 651
Topeka, Kansas 66612

KENTUCKY
Department of Workers' Claims
1270 Louisville Road
Frankfort, Kentucky 40601

NEBRASKA
Workers' Compensation Court
Post Office Box 98908
Lincoln, Nebraska 65809

NEVADA
Department of Industrial Relations
1390 South Curry Street
Carson City, Nevada 98710

NEW HAMPSHIRE
Workers' Compensation Board
19 Pillsbury Street
Concord, New Hampshire 03301

NEW JERSEY
Division of Workers' Compensation
State Office Building, #381
Trenton, New Jersey 08625

NEW MEXICO
Workers' Compensation Division
Post Office Box 27198
Albuquerque, New Mexico 87125

NEW YORK
State Insurance Board
199 Church Street
New York, New York 10007

NORTH CAROLINA
Industrial Commission
430 North Salisbury Street
Raleigh, North Carolina 27611

NORTH DAKOTA
Workers' Compensation Bureau
4007 North State Street
Bismark, North Dakota 58501

OHIO
Bureau of Workers' Compensation
246 North High Street
Columbus, Ohio 43215

TEXAS
Industrial Accident Board
200 East Riverside Drive
Austin, Texas 78704

UTAH
Workers' Compensation Fund
Post Office Box 510250
Salt Lake City, Utah 84151

VERMONT
Dept. of Labor and Industry
120 State Street
Montpelier, Vermont 05602

VIRGINIA
Industrial Commission
Post Office Box 1794
Richmond, Virginia 23220

WASHINGTON
Dept. of Labor and Industries
General Administration Bldg.
Olympia, Washington 98504

WEST VIRGINIA
Workers' Compensation Board
601 Morris Street
Charleston, W. Virginia 25301

WISCONSIN
Workers' Compensation Bureau
Post Office Box 7901
Madison, Wisconsin 53707

WYOMING
Workers' Compensation Dept.
122 West 25th Street
Cheyenne, Wyoming 82002

CHAPTER FIFTEEN

How to Become a Private Investigator

To become a licensed private investigator, you should contact the State Board of Private Investigators and/or Security Guards in the capitol city of your state. They will send you the requirements for that particular state. However, most states are set up in the same general way, with only the education and experience differing.

For instance, to own a private investigation agency, you will have to demonstrate that you have a certain number of years experience as a police officer or private investigator. There will probably be an education requirement (high school or college) and a test covering the state's private investigation requirements will have to be passed. Once the requirements to own an agency are met, you will then have to prove that you have liability insurance, have filed with the state's comptroller's office and/or secretary of state's office, provide proof that you are bonded (where applicable), and possibly other requirements will have to be met.

If you do not qualify to own and/or manage a private investigation company, you will then have to consider being employed through a private investigation company so that you can gain the experience necessary to open your own agency. All private investigators have to have a clear criminal history, a clear character profile, and at least a limited amount of education (high school). After that, each agency can hire part or full-time investigators based on their regular hiring procedures.

Just because you do not have any law enforcement experience or anything similar, does not keep you from pursuing this industry. In my own agency, I tend to hire those subjects who do not have any law enforcement background. Police officers typically have a hard time developing their views on an investigation based on the private industry versus the criminal element. Just because you are good at investigating a crime scene does not mean that you will be able to provide the private sector an unbiased, conclusive investigation without bringing the criminal activity of the subject in to question. For instance, if you are investigating a subject to determine if they are actually injured due to a worker's compensation injury, and during the investigation you determine that the subject is apparently selling drugs, the insurance company probably does not care. They are concerned with their issues and may not have the legal ground to do anything about the criminal activity. Unfortunately, some former officers can't "let it go" and it becomes an issue.

Therefore, my advice would be to check with your state to see how you line up with their requirements and, then proceed along those lines to become licensed, if you so choose.

ABOUT THE AUTHOR

Kelly E. Riddle

Industry Experience: Mr. Riddle has more than 18 years of investigative experience and established Kelmar and Associates more than eight years ago in 1989. Prior to founding his own company, Mr. Riddle worked for two other private investigation companies including a nation-wide operation.

Prior Law Enforcement Experience: Prior law enforcement experience includes being a member of the SWAT Team, a Training Officer, Emergency Medical Technician, Evidence Technician, Arson Investigator, Traffic Investigator and Breathalyzer operator.

Education: B.S. degree in Criminal Justice from the University of North Alabama.

Other Credentials: Author of "Private Investigating Made Easy," "To Serve and Protect: The True Story," "The Art of Surveillance," "Find Out Fast," "Nursing Home Abuse Investigations," and "The Investigator's Internet Black Book." In addition, he has two video tapes and an Internet Investigation software program. Designated an expert in physical surveillance and insurance investigations by the National Association of Investigative Specialists (NAIS). Founder of the Association of Christian Investigators and the PI Institute of Education.

Acclamations: The National Association of Investigative Specialists (NAIS) selected Mr. Riddle as the "Investigator of the Year (1997-98)." The PI Magazine also listed Mr. Riddle as the "#1 PI in the Nation." In addition, Mr. Riddle has been listed as "one of the top surveillance experts in the United States today" by NAIS. He has also been called "one of the most successful private investigators in the State of Texas" by Thomas Publications. His book, "The Art of Surveillance" was chosen as the "Best Book of the Year for Surveillance Investigations" by the National Association of Investigative Specialists.

Speaking Engagements: Guest speaker and lecturer who has appeared on various TV and radio shows and has been published in numerous publications. Mr. Riddle consistently speaks at conventions held by the National Association of Investigative Specialists, the Texas Association of Licensed Investigators, the National Association of Licensed Investigators, the Louisiana Association of Investigative Specialists, the National Platform Association and other civic and industry groups. Mr. Riddle is certified as a continuing education instructor by the Texas Board of Private Investigators and the Texas Board of Insurance.

Membership: TALI, NAJS, NALI, ASIS, LAPI, ION, ACI.

To Contact our Office:

Write us at:	Kelmar and Associates 2553 Jackson Keller, Suite 200 San Antonio, Texas 78230
Call us at:	(210) 342-0509 or fax (210) 342-0731
Visit our web sites:	http://www.kelmarpi.com http://pimall.com/kelmar/kelly.html http://pimall.com/aci/aci.html
e-mail us at:	kelmar@stic.net

Book/Video Order Form

Private Investigating Made Easy	$14.95
To Serve and Protect: The True Story	$19.95
The Art of Surveillance	$19.95
(Book of the Year 1997-98 by Thomas Pub.)	
Find Out Fast: Instant Guide to Records	$19.95
Nursing Home Abuse Investigations	$19.95
The Internet Black Book	$19.95
Video: Private Investigating Made Easy	$39.95
Video: The Art of Surveillance	$39.95
Software: Internet on Demand	$39.95
(Investigations Using the Internet)	

To order any of the above, please call our toll-free number: (888) 873-1714. Note: Add $2.95 (each) for shipping and handling. Texas residents add 8% sales tax.

Total book/Video order: ....$ ____________

Texas residents, 8% sales tax ....$ ____________

Shipping/Handling ($2.95 each) ....$ ____________

Total amount enclosed:..................................$ ____________

Name:____

Address: ______________________________________

City, State Zip: __________________________________

Make check or money order payble to: Kelmar and Associates
2553 Jackson Keller, Suite 200
San Antonio, Texas 78230

For your convenience, we also accept MasterCard, Visa, or you can call our Toll-Free number:

1-888-873-1714